"Tamara Vukusic has a̶ ̶̶̶̶ ̶̶̶̶ ̶̶̶̶ ̶̶̶̶ ̶̶̶̶ obits and turning the̶n. ̶.̶.̶.̶.̶ ̶.̶.̶.̶g̶g̶.̶.̶.̶ ̶.̶.̶ ̶g̶ humour. Life lessons from the obituaries. A decadent dissection of lives lived by characters whose habits and philosophies are worth emulating. A gentle reminder that it's not our salaries or credentials that define us."

— *Shelley Joyce, CBC Daybreak Kamloops*

****

"'Life Lessons from the Obituaries' is a funny and smart read that turns a popular pastime into witty life advice. Vukusic's First Person essay was one of the column's much-loved reads and still sends me to the obit pages to read between the lines, looking for perspective, strength and interesting people."

— *Catherine Dawson March, The Globe and Mail*

****

"Obittersweet" is thoughtfully written and surprisingly uplifting. The reader is provided with insights into the social worlds of others, including Vukusic's endearingly eccentric life. We see how the individuals are shaped by their circumstances, then the choices they made, the unique personalities they developed, and the legacies they left.

I am particularly fond of the reflection questions and imagine them as family conversation starters — a teen and/or adult version of Vukusic's *Spark Story Starter* cards.

— *Heather Parrott, Associate Professor of Sociology at Long Island University*

obittersweet

obittersweet

Life Lessons from Obituaries

Tamara Macpherson Vukusic

With gratitude,

Tamara Vukusic

Library and Archives Canada Cataloguing in Publication

Title: Obittersweet : life lessons from obituaries / by Tamara Macpherson Vukusic

Names: Vukusic, Tamara Macpherson, 1971- author

Identifiers: Canadiana (print) 20200346709 | Canadiana (ebook) 20200347012 | ISBN 9781771615280 (softcover) | ISBN 9781771615297 (PDF) | ISBN 9781771615303 (EPUB) | ISBN 9781771615310 (Kindle)

Subjects: LCSH: Obituaries.

Classification: LCC PS8643.U39 O25 2020 | DDC C814/.6—dc23

Published by Mosaic Press, Oakville, Ontario, Canada, 2020.

ONTARIO ARTS COUNCIL
CONSEIL DES ARTS DE L'ONTARIO
an Ontario government agency
un organisme du gouvernement de l'Ontario

Funded by the Government of Canada
Financé par le gouvernement du Canada

Canadä

We acknowledge the Ontario Arts Council for their support of our publishing program.
We acknowledge the Ontario Media Development Corporation for their support of our publishing program.

MOSAIC PRESS

1252 Speers Road, Units 1 & 2, Oakville, Ontario L6L 5N9

info@mosaic-press.com • www.mosaic-press.com

*To all the people who pour their hearts into writing
a life story, and especially to those who wrote
the obituaries that live on in this book.
Thank you for sharing your loved one with us.*

*For my Métis grandmothers who passed down through
stories the stuff that really matters. Names and dates
prescribed by European husbands are etched on paper,
but the mettle and grit of these women live on inside me.*

Table of Contents

Introduction

I have an odd ritual. I spend Saturday mornings with a coffee in one hand and the obituaries in the other. I have turned my obsession into an art, scanning for ink that lures with promises of quirks and vulnerabilities. Stuff that gets to the grit of a person, rather than the window-dressing of their professional titles. Mitch had *Tuesdays with Morrie.* I have Saturdays with the dead. These weekend coffee dates have provided me with guidance, validation, encouragement and sometimes a belly laugh. I started this weekly tradition in my 20s and two decades later I'm still at it.

Every week delivers new life lessons, often from people whose life is nothing like my own. I always feel grateful that I still have time to use what I learn from them in my own life. What a gift to discover a lesson nestled in a life story, illuminating what was valued and admired most about a person, all the salient bits distilled to a smaller word count than an elementary school essay. In the pages of this book I share some of these gifts with you.

This collection of 120 micro-biographies are those of ordinary people. People like you and me. "Great parent," "loving spouse" and "good friend" are common attributes noted in the obituaries. But there are so many ways to live a life. It stands to reason that what one leaves behind can take different forms.

An obituary usually introduces us to a person through the eyes of their loved ones. I wrestle with whether or not this conveys the whole truth of a person. It couldn't possibly, could it? After someone dies, they live on through the perceptions and memories of others. What others choose to remember becomes who they were. I often wish the person being remembered had the opportunity to read their own obituary. Can we be brave enough to write the obituary of a loved one while they are still living and share it with them like a love letter?

Reading the obits is like wandering the halls of a gallery, admiring a collection of interesting portraits. A few are elaborate, done in oil, with thick, gilded frames. Others are modest sketches. Some are bright caricatures full of quirky details. When I turn to my own canvas, I can try to emulate a shade of aquamarine from one or the curve of a line that caught my eye in another. My painting may be less measured, more conformist, less sophisticated, more outlandish. In the end, or at the end, it will reflect my own style, with glimpses of what I learned from the masters.

This collection of obit excerpts and life lessons is organized into monthly themes because life and death are inextricably connected to time. It has been said that who we meet is all about timing. Thanks to obituaries, the right people and the right words can find us even after they are gone.

On Saturday mornings I welcome these people — now numbering in the thousands — into my home. I applaud the beauty they found in the routine, the value they placed on experiences that didn't come with framed certificates, and their ability to laugh at themselves. They have helped me navigate, plot, placate and activate. I'm pretty sure I'm a better person thanks to them.

Why would a 20-year-old read obituaries?

I started reading the obits in my early 20s. I was working as the communications officer for The Perley and Rideau Veterans' Health Centre in Ottawa. The best part of my job was my time with the residents and patients. Every lunch hour for two years, Word War II Veteran and resident Lionel Lalonde wheeled his way into my office to deliver a french lesson. James Shepherd and I read to each other from our secret poetry notebooks at the end of my workdays. Peggy Taylor fed my reverence for military women with her Second World War stories of parachuting out of an airplane with her *"evening sandals"* tied around her neck so that she could *"pretty up"* and go the pub to extract information from soldiers. I felt the loss of each of these residents profoundly. I regularly turned to the obits to seek details of their funeral service. I would find myself lost in the life stories of these people, feeling gratified when their spirit was captured, scribbling additional details in the margins. I was almost always surprised to learn something that left me yearning to go back in time to ask more questions.

So began my obituary reading ritual that has continued for more than two decades.

How to read this book

When I read an obituary, I turn the words over in my mind, often discovering a life lesson in the process. This book is based on 120 obituaries chosen from the thousands I have read over twenty-plus years. It is organized into twelve chapters reflecting the twelve months of the calendar year. The life lessons gleaned from these obituaries are woven around the monthly themes and presented in three parts:

Part 1 is an excerpt from an obituary published in a Canadian newspaper.

Part 2 weaves a combination of facts from the obituary with research to contemplate the narrative more deeply. I often take an imagined sojourn beyond the confines of those facts and draw parallels to my own life experiences.

Additional excerpts pulled from the obituary appear in italicized quotation marks.

Part 3 is a question that invites you to reflect on your own life.

Within the pages of this book I hope you will recognize glimpses of your own life, qualities you'd like to cultivate, and strengths and quirks about yourself (and those you love) that are worthy of celebration. But above all, I hope you enjoy the read.

Why obituaries matter

Not everyone is remembered with an obituary. Many Indigenous Peoples favour oral tradition and ceremony over a written tribute. The same is true of other people around the globe.

Publishing an obituary often requires money and a person to do the writing. People without means or who are estranged from family often go unheralded, but not for lack of a story to tell. Having spent time searching for details about my own grandfather who grew up in an orphanage in England, I can attest that some family trees have whole limbs missing.

I've been exploring the reasons for which people write an obituary. They include honouring a person's life, informing a community, closure for loved ones and inviting others to attend a memorial service or extend sympathies. But there is one reason that caught me by surprise: obituaries serve as a public record for the sake of genealogy.

One of my all-time favourite obits makes no mention of a birth date or names of the spouse and children. It is a series of snippets that tell the story of a mother who worked hard and loved even harder. The only information that pins the obituary to a particular person is a name.

I often ask myself; which matters more? Passing on a family name? Contributing the gene for eye colour? The 50/50 odds of passing on artistic ability? Or is it the unique traits and perspectives that develop over a lifetime? What is the essence of a person, unique as their fingerprint?

We can't choose what we inherit, but these bits of humanity are something we can admire, covet, hold close and even try to emulate (or strengthen our resolve to do the exact opposite). Does it matter whether we share their surname? If we were inspired and moved only by humans with whom we share a thread of DNA, would we continue to uphold and celebrate Terry Fox, Martin Luther King, Jr. or Malala Yousafzai in classrooms across our country?

The perceived value of artwork often escalates after an artist dies. So too do our memories of a loved one once they are gone. As humans we treasure things that are hard to acquire, and this includes moments with another person.

We don't have to be related to, or even know, the people staring back at us in portraits to recognize their beauty, or courage or foibles. Likewise, anyone can glean something valuable from the way another person lived their life — what the person was willing to fight for, what they valued, or what gave them joy.

Perhaps we can add "life lessons for the living" as a reason for why people write — and read — obituaries.

New Year's Revolution:
Celebrate what you already do

JANUARY

To heck with New Year's Resolutions. Only eight percent of Canadians keep them anyway. What do you already do that is worthy of celebration?

In 2020 the most common New Year's resolutions were to eat healthier, exercise more and save money. I can't recall an obituary that remembers a person for achieving any of these things. The eight percent that kept their resolutions probably felt pretty good and maybe even dropped a pant size, but is that what really matters?

Time spent doing what you love to do with the people you love to do it with becomes the tangible, lasting part of what you leave behind. It becomes your legacy, and perhaps the blueprint that alters the way something is done long after you are gone.

It isn't the number of bench press repetitions or dollars banked for which each of the following ten people are admired and remembered. Let them shed light on what you could celebrate now, and what will be celebrated about you long after you are gone.

This year, rather than crafting a New Year's resolution, consider reflecting on what you already do that is worth celebrating. Resolve to live your life in a way that when you are gone, people notice something unique and precious missing.

Honour individuality

Aida Maria Ambery (1957–2015)

"Her children were a great joy in her life. She always celebrated their unique natures — and their choices."

This same appreciation for the individuality of others was reflected in her *"wide range of eclectic close friends."*

This trait must have made Aida an excellent mental health outreach worker. *"She knew all her clients by name, and most of them knew hers."* She showed others that she valued the unique characteristics that set them apart by remembering them. She made sure they felt seen.

I am constantly reminded that kids aren't mini versions of their parents. The fact that I enjoy a crowd, chaos and spontaneity has no bearing on whether or not our kids do. One of the hardest parts about parenting for me has been acknowledging my own assumptions and biases, and then trying to let them go.

Nowhere is this more evident than in the video footage taken in the 24 hours after our first son was born. My husband slicks our newborn's erratic flock of red hair into a rooster comb and hollers "*cock-a-doodle-doo*" loudly enough to prompt passer-by to poke their head in the door of our hospital room. I express my amusement loudly while holding the camera. We are both oblivious to the attempts of our son to turtle into his receiving blanket. Sixteen years later, he is still showing me the value of gauging the mood of a room before bursting in like the Kool-Aid Man.

Aida made space for others with an "*incredible gentleness, kindness and acceptance of others.*" But that didn't mean she was a wallflower. She was also known to blast an 80s tune and dance around the kitchen to kick off a dinner party. Aida has shown me that I can celebrate the individuality of others while staying true to what makes me unique.

What preset ideas do you have about the right way to live life that you can set aside when celebrating the people in your life?

Provide gathering places

The Rev. Walter (Paddy) Sellers (1919–2019)

> *"When he wasn't involved in re-building a church that had burned, or building a church to hold a growing congregation or updating a gracious older church or adding plumbing or new pews..."*

Paddy served as a minister with the United Church and led congregations in Manitoba, Ontario and Labrador. This hard-working man kept cattle and bees and built his own house, garage and barn. Paddy valued places because places hold people together. Many obituaries are dotted with references to gathering places: a church, a cultural centre, a family cottage or simply a welcoming home.

In a sea of new homes that have replaced front porches with car garages, we need more communal spaces. Spaces where exhausted parents with toddlers can commiserate, seniors living alone can find company and craft, teens can cut loose in safety and all of us can step out of our silos and be reminded that we are social creatures who need each other in countless ways.

In our house, teens are starting to frequent our family room and fridge. Sometimes they pull up a stool in the kitchen to talk about what's on their mind. My husband and I couldn't be more happy about this.

> *What can you do to make your home a place where people gather? What communal space can you lasso to help build a stronger sense of community?*

Bring immortal characters to life

Daryl Leonard Merle Sharp (1936-2019)

"Professor Brillig and Arnold will live on..."

Professor Brillig and Arnold are characters from Sharp's trilogy of Jungian primers, starting with *Chicken Little: The Inside Story.* Professor Brillig is Sharp's persona, a wise old man, and Arnold is his sidekick and shadow. Together, with a host of other characters, they take the reader on a spiritual journey of self-discovery.

Daryl was a teacher, writer, an editor and actor. His *"major labour of love"* was his publishing house — Inner City Books — dedicated to the work of Jungian psychology. The word "labour" is apt in reference to the 30 books he wrote. He gave birth to several much-loved book characters, including Professor Brillig and Arnold.

My Dad gave rise to immortal characters, too, not by writing books, but by inventing an imaginary boyfriend for each of his five daughters when we were young. I've never figured out why I got two (Ferd and Fred Dribbley). His brand of funny was goofball and this one hit the mark. Decades later these "boyfriends" still pursue us in the backdrop during visits with my sisters, and because they never took a breath, they will never be able to take a last one.

Have you created any imaginary characters through writing, storytelling or just poking fun? If they've made themselves scarce in recent years can you bring them back into your life and the lives of those you love?

Make sacrifices for a better tomorrow

Edris Josephine Whittle (1939–2019)

> *"In 1968, Edris sought new opportunities for her and her five children and immigrated to Toronto. She worked multiple jobs and endured harsh conditions to build a foundation for her family's life here. She retired as an employee of Suedemaster Leather in 2000. Throughout life's journey, Edris embodied respect, honesty and kindness despite not always receiving the same courtesy... She has instilled in her children and grandchildren the importance of education, perseverance and integrity throughout all of life's travels."*

The woman known as Teeny was *"born and grown"* in the hills of St. Thomas, Jamaica. She learned the value of hard work from an early age by tending to her father's farm while completing school. She was known to stand up to classmates who bullied her peers and was described as *"small in stature but fiercely vocal, if provoked."* Edris was 29 years old when she moved to Toronto with her five children to start a new life. It was 1968 and just three years after the last segregated school in Ontario closed. She was a visible minority in need of a job and a place to live with five dependents. It is thanks to the grit of people like Edris that Canada can boast being a mosaic where diversity is celebrated and inclusion is a way of life.

What risks would you take in search of a better life? How can you embrace and support those who choose Canada as their home?

Grow simple rituals with lasting magic

Maria-Louise Hincenbergs (1925-2019)

"Oma and maker of pancakes, pink stuff and Hallowe'en costumes."

Aside from dates, names of loved ones and Celebration of Life details, this is the one sentence in Maria-Louise's obituary that gives us a glimpse of who she was. But these ten words alone speak to the love and magic she brought to the lives of her five grandchildren. I can smell the stack of pancakes topped with a dollop of butter. I can see her sitting surrounded with scads of craft supplies, much of it in varying shades of pink with glitter in the mix. The steady thrum of her sewing machine offers a predictability that links visit to visit, year to year.

I vividly recall our son's drawing of our neighbour's swimming pool in response to the question posed by his Grade 2 teacher, "what was the best part of your summer?" This came on the heels of our most adventurous summer ever, with trips to South Carolina, New York City and Vancouver Island. We swam in our neighbour's pool just a few times that summer, usually in haste coming or going. Those of us parents who try to fill every moment of our kids' lives with life-enriching experiences could find comfort in realizing that what we remember is often the simple pleasures. We think it's the grand gestures and gifts that will make the difference or be remembered. This was an early reminder that we can provide experiences, but our kids are the only ones who can label them magic.

> *Ask those who matter most to you which memories they hold closest. You might be surprised. It may free you to revel in the simple things and invite them to take part. What do you do without fanfare that others might consider magic?*

Doodle your art out

Albert Arthur (Ab) Ablett (1935-2015)

"Art: 'I am not an artist ... I am just a doodler.' This is true. He was a renowned 'doodler' and many placemats and napkins in restaurants fell victim to his graphic tags. The instant he sat down in a restaurant, especially one with a paper placemat, out would come the pen. A broad white space would soon turn into an elaborate landscape, with mice and birds, old logs and trees: perhaps an outhouse or a cabin; maybe a lake or a brook. But before the meal came, there would be a new piece of art in the room.

Ab would always dismiss them, just flipping the placemat over again when the food arrived, but more likely than not, with the meal came a new placemat, this one intended for its common purpose and not the canvas of an artist, the adorned placemat whisked away and shown around the room.

Ella recalls, 'One time we were travelling, and I looked at this art hanging on the wall in the restaurant. It was a drawing of Ab's that he had drawn on the back of the restaurant's placemat during some previous trip and they had framed it. In the corner it said $75'."

Ab did what he loved to do surrounded by people he loved in an uneventful way. He didn't wait for large swaths of time to sequester himself in a studio with expensive supplies. He doodled for the joy of creating, whenever the opportunity presented itself. Of course there is great value in making the time and space to create, and honouring your work with quality supplies. But how many creative people go to their grave still waiting for the "right" time?

Ab reminds us that we need little more than a piece of paper (or placemat) and something to draw with, to access a place deep within and leave our mark. The bonus? More time for being with the people we love and a little ego-stroking along the way.

> *What do you love doing that can be done without fancy supplies or compromising time with the people you love?*

Let others know they matter

Roderick Milne MacKay (1936-2012)

> *"He never forgot a birthday and he arrived each year on the beach in Parksville with new kites, balls, shovels, buckets and more often than not, crazy hats or embarrassing t-shirts."*

Rod remembered birthdays and he was attentive to the people he cared for 365 days of the year. *"He was a talented artist who would work late into the night painting banners to recognize milestones in the lives of others."* His celebration of others wasn't limited to ear-marked dates on the calendar. Instead Rod paid attention to what mattered most to others. But he did make a point of ratcheting up the magic around special occasions, and Christmas was his favourite. He spent days decorating the family home during the holidays and won numerous awards in recognition of this gift to his community.

I especially love learning that in addition to giving generously to others, Rod "*never forgot his family.*"

I am in awe of anyone who remembers birthdays. I have a lifelong friend who has never forgotten mine. She even celebrates my half-birthday which has its origins in our teenage years. I love that she continues to do this despite my lack of reciprocity. I would love to remember birthdays. Heck, I'd settle for knowing what today's date is. I hope I let others know they matter. Whatever form that takes it's neither predictable nor consistent. But one thing I've learned from obituaries is that we each have our own way of showing love.

Can you accept that a card or flowers, or even saying happy birthday on the right date, isn't the only way to express love? How do you let others know they matter?

Grow lovely growing old

Doris Mary Ross Sturdee (1923-2017)

> *"She aged with grace and dignity, relinquishing once treasured pastimes without unseemly displays of distress. She gave up driving. She gave up cross-country skiing. She gave up tennis. She gave up writing things down. But she never gave up her family or her legions of friends. She was funny that way."*

Doris lived life with gusto and didn't shy away from new experiences. Yet she knew when it was time to pack it in. She could have pulled out self-deprecating jokes to protect her ego or taken up air space with apologies for being too slow, but she didn't. Instead she simply opted out with grace and found other ways to spend time with the people she loved.

A framed cross-stitch of the poem "Let me grow lovely" by Karle Wilson Baker (1878-1960) hung in my grandparent's home and now it hangs in mother's home. I remember reading it as a teenager and agreeing that old things *did* grow more lovely over time, including my grandmother who always smelled good (White Shoulders perfume), sparkled with rhinestone broaches and spooned her soup away from her.

Let me grow lovely, growing old—

So many fine things do:

Laces, and ivory, and gold,

And silks need not be new;

And there is healing in old trees,

Old streets a glamour hold;

Why may not I, as well as these,

Grow lovely, growing old?

In what ways will you choose to grow more lovely with the passing of time? Can you emulate the people and things around you that are evolving with grace as you grow older?

Give beyond your family and peers

Barbara "Jean" Godden (1928–2016)

"Jean's heart was as big and deep as the ocean she grew up beside. Many times in the life of her family she provided shelter to her children's friends who were alone and lost in the world."

Among many other attributes, Jean is referred to as a *"nurturer supreme."* She must have had lots of opportunities to exercise this superpower as a nurse, mother, grandmother and lifelong friend. I imagine her swooping in with a freshly laundered blanket for her patients and warming up her hands before changing a dressing. I see her doing up the top button of the winter coats of visitors before they head out into the blowing winter snow. She probably packed an extra brown bag lunch and laundered the clothes of kids that were not her own, never bringing attention to her offering.

I think most of us can think of an adult who helped us in our childhood years, even if it was as simple as setting out an extra place at the dinner table. One Christmas Eve my mom and I wandered down to sit on the swings at the nearby community centre after a bowl of Kraft Dinner in our loving but quiet home. On the way back home I got the courage to knock on the door of a good friend from school. His family invited us to join them in their twinkling carol-filled home, followed by a candlelight service at their church. This became a tradition that continued until we graduated from high school and I value it deeply to this day. Over-scheduled kids and adults, homes with garages in place of the long-lost front porch, and digital devices that swallow us whole, make it harder to remember the young people that are alone and lost. But those young people need us, and Jean has reminded us.

Who could you put out an extra plate for at your table? Who needs some words of support? To whom can you give your ear? Or to whom can you simply listen?

Be a good sport

Wm. Gordon Bacon (1944-2019)

"For many years, Gord held the distinction of holding the highest individual ranking for a Canadian fly fisherman in world competition. When this standing was eclipsed, he couldn't have been more proud and excited for the former team-mate who took over this distinction."

In addition to competing for his country in *"countless international competitions"* as a long-standing member and captain of the Canadian Fly Fishing team, Gord achieved a doctorate in metallurgic engineering. He became well-established as an expert and mentor in his field and founded Bacon Donaldson Associates, which grew to employ seventy-five individuals. Although his career and personal pursuits are impressive, Gord felt *"his greatest achievement was the number of enduring friendships he formed and maintained during his life."* With the thread of good sportsmanship that ran through his approach to both his personal and professional life, it comes as no surprise that he made and kept many friends in his lifetime.

I like to imagine Gord congratulating his newly minted record-holding teammate with a fist bump before moving in for a bear hug. If we follow Gord's example and graciously relinquish roles and titles with remarkable sportsmanship we show others that we are on everyone's team. Gord went beyond good sportsmanship and felt "*proud and excited*" for the achievement of his team-mate, even when it meant stepping off the podium.

Whose success can you champion and celebrate even if it eclipses your own?

Move over Tinder

Lovers have been finding each other for centuries without the help of an app. We may imagine that in yesteryear people found their soul mate on a church pew under the kaleidoscope of stained glass windows or doing the twist on Sadie Hawkins Day in the high school gym. But the snippets from the obituaries in this chapter are proof that you might find your soul mate in the least expected place, without the help of eHarmony.

An added bonus? Any relationship that is noted in an obituary endured the test of time and was valued. The average length of the relationships found in this section is 55 years.

Hollywood would have us believe that when romance finds us we are either instantly seized by mutual adoration or the feeling is one-sided, sending the smitten one on a relentless pursuit until the disinterested experiences a change of heart. We rarely hear about the reality: the slow burn. For most of us, reality consists of clumsy pick-up lines, awkward first kisses and quasi-ambivalent beginnings that morph into a lifetime of love and partnership.

Each one of these people met their life partner while they were busy living life, long before the worldwide net widened their scope of possibility. I know of several solid romantic relationships that are part of the 40 percent that began online. But that requires looking. If you stop looking for love is it possible that love might find you instead?

Grab their attention

John Sherman Bleakney (1928-2019)

> *"From an early age, Sherman loved the outdoors and developed
> an interest in herpetology, the study of reptiles and amphibians.
> Story has it that to first get the attention of his future wife,
> Nancy Tyler, a fellow biology student at Acadia University, he
> put a frog down her lab coat."*

Sherman and Nancy were married for 45 years. You may think this
attention-grabbing incident was impulsive, but it notes in his obit
that, "*Sherman's motto throughout life was 'always anticipate'. Things
had to be planned in advance and well done.*" Putting a frog down
Nancy's lab coat was either a rare spontaneous act for Sherman, or
a premeditated act of courtship. All that matters is that he got her
attention. And then won her affection.

They spent their honeymoon camping through Ontario, Quebec
and the Maritimes, collecting and documenting frogs and
turtles and snakes along the way, culminating in the book, *A*

Zoogeographical Study of the Amphibians and Reptiles of Eastern Canada.

Sherman took the position of Curator of Herpetology at the National Museum in Ottawa in the early 1950s. He returned to Wolfville in 1957 to accept a biology professorship at the very university where he met Nancy. It was back in Wolfville that Sherman dissected a leatherback sea turtle in the midst of Nancy's beautiful English perennial garden because it was too large for the Acadia lab tables. Their children recount that Nancy insisted her garden had a *"vaguely oily fishy smell for years afterwards, much to her chagrin."* Sherman never stopped garnering her attention with his zest.

I met my husband in the cheese section of Northmart in Iqaluit, Nunavut. I was eight weeks into a two-year contract as the External Relations Manager of the 2002 Arctic Winter Games. He had just arrived to a six-week family medicine residency. I offered to take him out on the land on my new 440 Polaris snowmobile the next afternoon. After he climbed onto the back of my crotch rocket, I hit the gas. Hard. We flew so fast he flipped off the back and his boots fell off. We rolled around laughing in the snow with the smell of gas from a two-stroke engine wafting over us. This has become my most favourite smell ever. This one impulsive moment did the trick. We just celebrated 16 years of marriage.

> *Do you have a crush on someone you know? What impulsive act could you pull out to get their attention?*

An accidental spark

Mary Louise Watt (1932-2019)

"Mary Louise made the acquaintance of her future husband, David Watt, on shared Toronto Transit Commission bus rides on route 82. Their relationship started warming not long after David, delayed, sprinted to catch the bus. Watching from her seat she witnessed the young medical student flagging down the bus while running after it. And she watched his spark of realization as he stepped onto the bus discovering that he had, through friction, lit a pack of matches in his front left pants pocket. The accidental ignition kindled conversation and a closeness that would ultimately guide them through their lives together."

Neither Mary Louise nor David lived until their 64th wedding anniversary, but their children are going to mark the date with a celebration of life to honour both of them in June 2020. This is a testament to how deeply their children valued their parents' shared commitment to each other and their family.

What are the chances that a modern day Mary Louise would be looking out the window long enough to notice David frantically trying to flag down a bus? A whopping 95% of Canadian millenials (24-39 year-olds) own a smartphone and spend an average 3.2 hours on it each day.

Our daily routines provide repeat opportunities to meet those whose lives run parallel to ours. Maybe we just need to look up long enough to notice.

Are you willing to experience life unfold around you instead of looking down at your mobile device, book or paperwork, even for just a few minutes each day?

Old hands

Frederick Joseph Marker (1936-2019)

"After a long struggle with Parkinson's disease, Lise-Lone's death in 2013 marked a major turning point in Frederick's existence. 'That I ever regained my footing in life is thanks to my partner Anne Dupré,' he wrote in his class report for his 60th reunion at Harvard five years later. A chance encounter with the widow of a distinguished university colleague he had never met gave both Frederick and Anne a fresh new reason for living. 'Between us we have weathered 103 years of marriage and, as such, we are old hands at the routine' they liked to remind friends."

Frederick and Anne shared six years together. This obituary brilliantly upholds the sanctity of his 50-plus year marriage to Lise-Lone, while also honouring the value of the love that carried him through to his final days.

When reading an obituary I am sometimes stung by the reality that true love can be found again after a spouse dies. I know I shouldn't be, but I am. Imagining my husband in love with someone else isn't comfortable. But after reading this obituary it seems not only palatable, but important.

Can you accept that love doesn't lose value when two people can no longer be together? Can you accept that hearts can make space for more love, even when they are already full to the brim?

Lay pipe together

Dennis James Fonso, (alias Foxy) (1950–2019)

"Dennis met his wife, Michele Fitzmaurice, when they worked together on the Trans Canada pipeline. Their work relationship blossomed into a romance that led to 32 years of marriage and a beautiful daughter, Meghan (Dennis' mini-me and sidekick)."

This story reminds us that working with someone at a job has many of the same elements as working together as romantic partners: trust, communication and team work. Neither Dennis nor Michele had to wrestle with reconciling an online bio or a touched-up photo to get to the heart of who they each were. I imagine them working side-by-side hoisting heavy equipment with words of encouragement bouncing back and forth between them like a ping-pong ball. I wonder if they busted a gut sharing inside jokes about their workmates on their dates.

According to a 2019 study, office romances are more likely to lead to marriage than relationships started in any other way. Another study found that a whopping one in three office relationships result in marriage, yet only 16 percent of people meet their romantic partner at work. In *The Anatomy of Love*, Helen Fisher confirms "At work, one's partner or spouse is nowhere visible, except perhaps as a photo on a desk. Office mates often share the same schedules, deadlines and anxieties, even the same mealtime, food and dress code."

Can you find common threads with your work mates that strengthen your bond? If you aren't looking for romance can you make space for one more friend?

Father knows best

Catherine Margaret Buchanan (1924-2019)

"That very same year, 1939, Dunoon experienced an unusually chilly winter replete with snow, a rarity. Fortuitous weather, as it transpired. One afternoon, the hills of Dunoon covered in a blanket of fresh snow, a certain Herbie Buchanan and a mate took to tobogganing. Spying them from her kitchen window young Kay told her dad what fun they must be having. Well, her dad marched her right out and introduced her to young Herbie. Of course, Herbie was smitten with such a clever lass. Then and there began a 70-year love affair uninterrupted until Herb's passing a few years ago."

I wonder if there were quips around the dinner table about this being an arranged marriage. Kay's Dad must have delighted in knowing he was partially responsible as he watched these two fall in love. I can see him turning a blind eye to the squeak of the front door as young Kay crept in past curfew. The smile meandering across his face while sneaking a peak through the curtain as Herbie hovered a little too long at the door stoop after a date. And what was his response when Herbie asked him for his daughter's hand in marriage? I bet he "whooped."

This simple scenario is laden with promise. Unfortunately this is a hard one to replicate, but perhaps the lesson is that a bit of meddling has its place.

> *Can you roll with it when you are unexpectedly introduced to a new person? If you aren't in the market for romance, you can instead play the role of cupid: seize a moment to make introductions for an unlikely pair.*

Be relentless

June Marie Rosaleen Kidman Ainley (1924-2019)

"In the early days of WWII, June was a teenager living in Bury, West Sussex. Just out of boarding school, she was training to join the war effort as part of the Wrens (Women's Royal Naval Service), where she would specialize in directing landing planes with the Fleet Air Arm, a post reserved for young ladies with 'good strong voices.' One day, June was hitchhiking home from training when a handsome Canadian soldier stopped his motorcycle. Patrick Ainley offered her a ride home. Young romance fluttered, but wasn't to flourish until he returned from the Italian front five years later. In 1945, June scoured the newspaper for names of displaced soldiers and managed to locate Patrick, who had been discharged in Sicily having come down with pneumonia. She nursed him back to health and the rest, as they say, was history. June and Patrick were married at St. George's Hanover Square, London, in September of 1946."

They were married for 44 years. *"June and Patrick's passion and respect for one another never dwindled, and when Patrick died of cancer in 1990 June was distraught."*

It's incredibly romantic to learn that a fleeting moment held enough weight to cement two people five years later. I admire that it was June who tracked down Patrick, as we all too often imagine the handsome soldier pursuing his future young bride. Did June bury her head in the back of his neck and breath him in as he rode his motorcycle on the day of their brief first encounter? Did the heat from Patrick's body keep her warm as she gripped around his chest with the wind whipping past? Was his smell familiar to June when they reunited five years later?

The lesson could be to throw caution to the wind when meeting a handsome stranger. Or, it could be to honour your first instinct (or flutter), and then to stay the course with your interest until you seal the deal.

> *It's easier to find people with the advent of social media. If you wanted to track someone down whom you met only briefly, would you be willing to try to find them June's old-fashioned style? What would this look like?*

Sing together

Charles "Stormin" Norman Atkinson (1928-2019)

"The man loved to sing — not surprising, he met Grace when they were both involved in the Operatic Society in Regina. They were married in 1953 and then the family arrived. Four little girls in five years and five years later one more! Norm and Grace were always involved in the church choir, and they got their girls singing together at the local competitions. Norm would direct and Grace played the piano and many little musicals were produced at church in Regina and Kamloops."

The obit proudly notes that, *"Norman and Grace were married for 66 years and 16 days!"* Norm encouraged his family, friends and mere acquaintances to *"come on, just give it a try."* That might have been a blanket statement for Norm, but I hear him telling us to get out there and find someone to love or something we love to do. And if you don't already have a soft spot for Stormin' Norm, I will share one more line from his obituary to reel you in. *"He*

went to clown school when he finished plumbing, and entertained
kids wherever he went."

My sister swears by the adage "couples who play together stay
together," referring to the sports — windsurfing and sailing —
she enjoys with her husband. If this is true, it must also apply to
a shared love of the arts in its many forms. I've come across a
long and curious list of interests shared by couples while reading
the obituaries: painting, acting, doing the jive and even toaster-
oven gourmet cooking.

What shared interests can you and your partner cultivate
together? What club, group or activity can you join to
meet others with similar interests, be it romantic or just
friendly?

Underwhelming first encounters

Charles William "Bill" Cooper (1926-2019)

> *"Bill had briefly met Marj Lewis in Jasper in 1953 and they instantly disliked each other. After reconnecting in 1964, they eloped on a locomotive. They raised their family in Kamloops, BC, where they lived for 40 years before moving to Calgary in 2006."*

I appreciate the honesty of this obituary. I appreciate that their first meeting is something Bill and Marj could laugh at. But I mostly appreciate the reminder that so much about life is timing and circumstance. Bill and Marj are a testimony to the importance of reconsidering first impressions. Their 55 years together is proof of the rewards we stand to reap when we keep an open mind and an open heart.

Can't you picture them giddy with excitement sitting on the train as the shrill whistle announced the start of their journey together? Can you hear the lethargic chug of the wheels quickly picking up pace to match their determined charge forward as a married couple? Bill was the engineer the day they travelled from Jasper to Edmonton to elope, with Marj right beside him. She sat in the same seat on Bill's final run before retirement 27 years later.

I am somewhat relieved when I hear a story that defies love at first sight. Maybe because it has never happened to me.

Isn't it the folly of humans to have a brief spell-binding encounter that propels one to fill in the blanks with imagined conversations and romantic interludes? Who can possibly live up to the character we construct? It would seem that a slow burn fuelled by real-time encounters has a better chance of success.

If single, have you met anyone that underwhelmed you at first, who you might reconsider? If married, did your partner possess any traits you originally thought would be deal breakers?

Uncanny Coincidences

Terence Patrick O'Donelan Bredin (1929-2020)

"He knew our mother was his perfect match when they discovered that each of their fathers was missing an arm — a farming accident in one case and a fall from a crowded railway platform during WWI the other."

Not long after Terence arrived at Upper Canada College (UCC) in Toronto to teach Latin and Ancient Greek, he met his wife-to-be Elizabeth who was working as a helper to the school nurse, Miss Bee. On first read, the telling of this uncanny coincidence which led Terence to believe Elizabeth was his "perfect match" seems sweet and maybe a little naive. It's in their discovery of this coincidence that the start of their love story is nestled.

Finding the common threads we share with another person requires the kind of thoughtful questions and earnest listening that can happen only when we are in with both feet. When we want to find those threads, they reveal themselves.

I love to imagine the early exchanges between the young Terence and Elizabeth during brief stolen moments when no one was looking, or affectionately spilled into discreetly delivered notes. In revealing themselves, little by little, at what point does one mention a father with only one arm? Were there tales of sympathy? Admissions of embarrassment? Followed by the astonishment of a shared claim to bragging rights?

Was it fate after all? The marriage of Terence and Elizabeth spanned 48 years. Their three adult children were touched by the tenderness Terence showed in caring for his ailing wife during their final ten years together before she died.

Terence returned to UCC to attend the school's former teachers and staff luncheon just months before he died. More than half a century had passed since his young and lasting love for Elizabeth unfurled in the very same hallways.

The first time my husband and I camped together it was on the tundra of Nunavut just beyond the outskirts of Iqaluit in 2000. We each pulled a 1980s North Face mummy-style sleeping bag from our pack. We managed to stay cool about the coincidence. But then we discovered that our bags zipped together, as only a right-facing mummy bag and a left-facing mummy bag can do. By the time we were eating alpine donuts and drinking coffee grounds we were talking about the life we would build together.

What coincidences have played a role in your major life decisions? What do you chalk up to coincidence that might instead be fate?

Second chances

Alex Berman (1924-2019)

"At a university function he met Val, proclaimed to friends he would one day marry her, but then proceeded to stand her up on their first date. Despite this, they were married in 1948."

Was he nervous? Did he get cold feet? Was he just forgetful? I suppose none of that matters. What *does* matter is that Val found it in her heart to give him another chance. And if this isn't a lesson for lifelong love, I don't know what is. The importance of her forgiveness is clear, *"After 71 years they continued to walk hand in hand, though the pace was just a little slower."*

I'm afraid I'm the Alex in the equation. I orchestrate entire conversations, gestures, letters and events in my mind that never come to fruition. They are fuelled by good intentions but fall short in execution. I have yet to find a calendar or an agenda that can cure me. I greatly appreciate Val's demonstration of forgiveness and understanding. I am thankful for the "Vals" out there that take me at face value, even when my face doesn't appear.

> *Can you forgive the next person that lets you down but is sincerely sorry for doing so? More importantly, can you forgive yourself when you do the same?*

Love in full bloom

Dr. Melville Joseph Swartz (1912-2006)

> *"Back in Montreal, amid poetry and roses, he wed Ruby Rabinovitch in 1946."*

Ruby T. Swartz (1916-2010)

> *"Ruby and Mel shared a tender long lasting love. For 60 years, from their marriage in 1946, cards and flowers, poetry and fun flowed between them. They loved dancing. Until their last days, they attended the ballet, symphony, theatre and opera."*

Mel and Ruby cherished each other deeply and this expanded to encompass their three children. They backed and supported their children in every possible way, yet despite the rigorous demands of parenthood they made space for each other and actively fed their life-long romance.

She was "Dignified, mischievous, an optimist with a delightful sense of humour."

"He savoured good company, good conversation, good food, and good story."

She delighted and he savoured. They never stopped growing and developing, learning and loving. Together.

"Flowers, poetry and fun" flowed between Mel and Ruby for 60 years. Herein lies the secret to their life-long romance. Most of us associate these gestures with budding romance, in the early days of cheeks that flush involuntarily and dipping a toe in an imagined future together. Rightly so, but Mel and Ruby have shown us that you can cherish and savour every phase of love, from tight bud to full-blossom, even to the wilting and dropping of petals. Even after death love continues, as this poem written by Ruby for her "Mellie" shows.

"I tell of Life - this seed is love When first 'tis born with roots unseen, Until full blown, exquisite, rare! A bud to know - awakening."

How can you capture the intoxicating early days of romantic love as the years unfold? If romantic love is not on your radar, how can you keep your other important relationships playful and loving?

One sentence that magically sums

MARCH

I love a good quest. When I read the obits I hunt for small flecks of gold; short sentences that shimmer. I look for ones that, on their own, tell us what made a person distinctive. Sometimes it's a tightly crafted sentence that embodies their essence, other times a single fact that tells a story beyond the confines of words.

"Let memories surround you, a word someone may say,
Will suddenly recapture a time, an hour, a day."

Blessings and prayers are recognized at an Irish funeral as a part of healing. Carefully choosing words to honour a loved one gives us a tiny sense of control at a time when we often feel helpless. A line from the Irish funeral blessing "Feel No Guilt in Laughter" seems apropos here.

My husband and I haven't recorded the classic "firsts" of our kids. You know, first smile, first steps, or the loss of the first tooth. Instead we keep a small notebook of the things they say that make us laugh, leave us gobsmacked or lead us to reflect on how much they already understand about the world. We are amazed that one sentence brings back an entire interaction or afternoon, years after the fact. When I revisit their words I can hear their wild laughter, see their lower pouty lip or feel their stickiness.

Sometimes an economy of words forces us to distill a person's essence into a brief description that (almost) says it all. It turns out I'm not the only one obsessed with word counts. The Six-Word Memoir project launched by *Smith Magazine* is a global phenomena with more than one million people submitting their life story using only six words.

This chapter features sentences with 15 words or less. Nothing makes me appreciate the value of words more than when they leave me missing someone I've never met.

If you had only 15 words to sum up what you want to be remembered for, what would they be? How about 15 words to convey what matters to you most?

Fifteen words

Derek Macdonald Foulds (1923-2019)

"Derek made life fun, whether it was doing the dishes or sailing on Georgian Bay."

Can you picture Derek having fun as he washed dishes? Goading the dish dryer to keep pace, doling out points for an empty dish drainer, docking points when dishes amass? Laughing, flicking the dishtowel at unsuspecting critics? How about the family road trips to Georgian Bay—with two kids in the back seat, noses pressed to window, scanning the highway for a bicycle (1 point!), tent trailer (2 points!), or canoe (3 points!). It's easy to make a full-throttle adventure fun. But finding fun in washing dishes? Engaging kids for hours on a road trip without iPads? Now that's someone who knows how to make life fun.

Where can you find fun in a task that might also be boring, frightening or pure skull-drudgery?

Fourteen words

Kenneth Joseph Alexander Vallilee (1943–2019)

"He left the world like he left most social engagements, abruptly and too soon."

We all know a Kenneth. If we choose to not take their actions personally we can admire them for their honesty and unapologetic boundary-setting. I wonder if Ken had perfected the Irish goodbye; sneaking out of a party without telling anyone so that you can avoid the awkward, half-in-half-out-the-door conversations.

> *How do you exit a party? Do you prefer the Irish goodbye or the long drawn-out kind that Hollywood movies are made of?*

Thirteen words

Hugh Alexander MacNicol (1933–2019)

"Nobody liked a good laugh more than Hugh and his laugh was legendary."

I imagine a "legendary laugh" to be both frequent and distinct. Apparently it was loud enough to land Hugh in hot water with his teachers on several occasions. Does the laugh of someone you know come to mind? I can't help but think of my husband on one of our first dates getting ribbed by a comedian for his "girl laugh." The fact that his ego wasn't bruised made me swoon even more.

The memory of laughter is a legacy worth leaving. Can you see it as the gift it is? Do you know anyone with a "legendary laugh"?

Twelve words

George Brady (1928–2019)

"The family continued to grow with badly trained but much loved dogs."

Reading this I envision a happy and accepting home busting at the seams. A place where self-effacing humour is valued and no one takes themselves too seriously.

I appreciate knowing there are other families that understand good behaviour and genuine love can be mutually exclusive.

> *What shortcoming could you reframe as a strength? A messy house where kids can create with abandon? A hobby that leads to permanent stains on the cabinet fronts and sink faucets? Jokes so bad they become endearing? An overzealous adventure that is so uncomfortable you will never forget it?*

Eleven words

Ina Perry Weldon (1926-2017)

"Ina's joy, humour, mischief and love opened doors, dried tears, hatched a plan, tickled and inspired."

Each of these short snippets about Ina say so much. I see a mom who opened doors for a brood of children that skipped beside her down the street and, when they were older, counselled them through disappointments. I see a friend who dried tears with compassionate silence and a tissue some days, and who offered straight-from-the-hip advice on others. Hatching plans? Tickling? Inspiring? This is yet another person I feel sad to have lost.

This obit also reminds me that love is a verb, which often expresses itself in action: kick, paint, eat. It shows how, through a lifetime, we weave relationships with small give-and-take interactions.

What plans can you hatch, whose tears can you dry? What door can you open for someone else?

Ten words

J. Alexander Langford Q.C. (1931–2019)

"He patiently acted as the family Google to the end."

Alex must have known a great deal about almost everything. To "patiently act as the family Google" suggests that he was willing to entertain questions at the whim of others rather than extol his knowledge freely.

I avoid *Trivial Pursuit* at all costs and make frequent returns to my cookbook when baking. Was that baking soda or baking powder? Return to recipe, back to bowl; soda or powder? You get the idea. I am in awe of brilliant people like Alex.

> *What do you do imperfectly that gives others (who do it very well) the opportunity to look like a genius? On the other hand, what resource do you patiently provide that helps others through their day?*

Nine words

Hilda Amy MacQuarrie (1921-2006)

"Thanks for the firm hand; thanks for letting go."

This is exactly how I would like to be thought of as a parent; fully present and supportive but also nudging our kids towards independence to become capable humans. All this, and more, is expressed in these nine words.

I'm pretty sure I've finally got the firm hand part figured out. It's the letting go I haven't sorted through yet.

> *Have you ever let go in the name of love? How do you find balance between holding on and letting go?*

Eight words

Keiko Margaret Lyons (1923-2019)

"She was pig-headed, optimistic, funny and fearless."

I wouldn't have thought that "pig-headed" could work in an obituary, but here it works brilliantly. Besides, it's hard not to admire someone who fiercely holds their ground for what they believe is right.

> *Assuming the obit writer knows you well, what qualities, flattering or not, could be used to describe you best?*

Seven words

David Grant Martin (1939-2019)

"David listened acutely, with his whole being."

David Grant Martin's obituary was sent to me by one of my closest friends. Martin had been his psychology professor and Ph.D. mentor at University of Manitoba. My friend was deeply affected by the loss of David and shared several stories that make me feel as if I had met this man who mastered the art of human connection. I may be biased, but I love this seven-word sentence because it encapsulates much of what made David remarkable. His fully engaged listening showed others that his mind was open to their ideas. It let others know they were valued. David said so much with no words. He spoke volumes with his ears and attention rather than his mouth.

How can you listen with your whole being?

Six words

Johanna Helfinger (1930-2019)

"Mom's self-education was haphazard but impressive... Her burning curiosity about the world was passed on to her children and created a climate supportive of learning within the home."

Having read Johanna's obituary more times than I will admit, I can confirm this sentence could not be more perfect. Johanna learned Latin by making friends with a local priest; she explored Ireland vicariously by seeking out Irish people; she was both superstitious and pan-religious. She read scholarly books about the Middle Ages, geography and English literature; and while still working at a physically demanding job, she took Italian courses at University of Waterloo. Her two children were the first in the family to earn post-graduate degrees for which they credit Johanna.

Have you ever been motivated to study for the sake of learning rather than for a certificate to hang on the wall?

Five words

Holly Denny Chercover (1963-2019)

"She was the frog whisperer."

Don't you want to know more? I do. Because anyone who makes a point of "using body language and gentle vocal encouragement rather than physical contact" (yes, I looked up the definition of "whisperer") with a frog is my kind of person. I would have liked to sit with Holly in her garden, frogs croaking in the background, seeing her belly down on the ground face-to-face with one of her green friends.

> *Are you a whisperer? To whom or what can you give "gentle vocal encouragement?"*

Fools make their mark

We don't expect to find humour in the obituaries, which is part of why it's so darn awesome when we do. Most of us enjoy making others laugh when we attempt a joke (and some of us enjoy making others laugh when we didn't mean to). So it stands to reason that making someone chuckle after we are gone is a coup.

I believe when we write an obituary for a loved one we write from somewhere between our view of them and how we think they viewed themselves. If in doing this we can let their humour shine through we have done them a great service. When an obituary is genuine and gets to the grit of the person we can hear their unique brand of funny; sarcastic, goofy, self-effacing, witty, someone who likes to stir the pot, or — my personal favourite — funny by accident.

An article in *The Guardian* addresses the role of birth order in humour. The opening line is "Youngest siblings are the funniest." Then comes the jab. Results from a British YouGov poll reveal that youngest siblings are more likely to *think* they are the funny. A whopping 46 percent of youngest siblings think they are the funniest of all the kids in their family.

The good news is there is no definition for "sense of humour," despite attempts by philosophers, psychologists and scientists to come up with one. This gives us a great deal of latitude to define "sense of humour" to suit our own funny bone.

"Happy families: A twin study of humour" measured the response of twins to cartoons. Findings suggest that humour is "largely influenced by the shared environment, with no significant contribution from genetic factors." It goes on to acknowledge that family, peers, teachers, religion, the media and politics likely play a role cultivating a sense of humour. In short, humour can be learned.

Humour is a shared experience. Maybe your role is humour connoisseur. Every fool needs an audience.

See if you can spot your brand of funny among the ten people featured in this chapter inspired by April Fool's Day. While they may have passed, their humour lives on.

The Clown

Roderick Milne MacKay (1936-2012)

"It was with the Shrine Clown Unit that 'Poor Rod' was born. 'Poor Rod', a sad clown fashioned after his childhood idol Emmitt Kelly, delighted parade goers across the province for more than three decades. Although 'Poor Rod' was his official clown persona, he always seemed to be clowning around. Whether it was a pair of crazy glasses or an outrageous outfit, if Rod thought he could get a laugh he would put it on."

"Poor Rod" was rooted in far more than laughs. Shriners are a brotherhood dedicated to providing care for children and families in need. They are bound by their desire to have fun *and* do good.

Rod's service as a Shriner spanned the last three decades of his more than fifty years of involvement with community service clubs. I am going to guess that Rod's membership with the

Shriners was planned because he founded the Clown Unit of the Cowichan Valley Shrine club just *one week* after becoming a member.

Rod's time as a clown wasn't limited to when he donned his face paint and wig. He was a *"skilled prankster." "Even if you'd been fooled before he could unwittingly draw you into his scheme until that moment when you knew you'd been had, at which point he would laugh with delight."* Even in his last days Rod continued to tell stories about his crazy antics from years gone by and chuckle as if they had just happened.

The same year Rod founded the Shriner's Clown Unit in Cowichan (1976), I experienced my first Shrine Circus. I was in kindergarten and my brother, who had just started junior high, was excited to treat me with his own money. He stopped at the concession and bought a box of pink candy popcorn for me. I squished the box sideways hoping I'd find a prize at the bottom. The entire pink contents cascaded over my shoes. A nearby clown looked at me, tilted his head in sympathy and honked his horn. My brother spent the bus fare for our ride home on a second box of popcorn. The walk home from downtown Winnipeg gave us hours to recount the antics of all the clowns, but the commiserating clown was, and always will be, my all-time favourite.

> *What good cause would you be willing to clown around for? How can you mix silly antics with giving to your community?*

The Rabble-rouser

William (Bill) Woodyatt (1950-2019)

*"Thankfully our parents (Joe and Doreen) broke the mould
when they made Bill almost better known as "Stumpy".
... To Jeff and I (Mari-Jayne) he was our big brother who
played hockey for the Marlies and raced cars. Either his own
car or, in his younger years, our father's, around the streets
of Don Mills in the middle of the night."*

Mari-Jayne picked the perfect time to tell on her brother
"Stumpy." It's much too late for repercussions from their parents.
Can you imagine the two younger siblings peeking out their
bedroom windows in their PJs as Stumpy slowly rolled their
parents car out of the driveway in neutral and then hit the gas
when the coast was clear? Did they give each other secret looks
at the breakfast table the next morning as Stumpy bragged about
the outstanding sleep he had?

At a close friend's wedding I told the story of the two of us taking out her parent's car when we were 15 (we were taking driving lessons together at the time). We drove around the block a few times and then narrowly missed knocking over a gas pump trying to get the gas gauge back to its original position. I assumed this would be a great wedding story. It turns out I should have waited until she was dead, like Mari-Jayne did for Stumpy.

What secret rabble-rousing have you done in your lifetime? If the answer is "none," I have some good news for you. You still have time! Which secrets would you rather take with you?

Tongue-in-Cheek Funny Guy

Herbert Mosses Duguay (1914–2015)

"Herb's first memory was seeing the World War I soldiers coming home in 1919. Around this time he was run over by a brand new Model T Ford. We are thankful for their high wheel clearance."

I love everything about these three short sentences; the brief history lesson, the image of the curious five-year-old Herbert getting a little too close to the action, and gratitude for a man who lived *"just short of 100 years"* with humour. All delivered with a good excuse to laugh.

I can't resist sharing another sentence about Herb that is equal parts funny and heartfelt; *"He built bombers at Fairchild Aircraft in Montreal during World War 2 because the army didn't want him. They said he had a bad heart. They were wrong. Herb was all heart."* This obituary is truly a love letter to Herb written by his daughter.

She has captured his kindness, self-effacing humour and an entire century of not taking himself too seriously in this beautiful obituary.

Some people choose to make light of events that end well but could just have easily ended in tragedy. It's the alternative to becoming overwhelmed by what could have been. I recall reading the words of Moliere on the wall of the Vancouver Art Gallery years ago: "Life is a tragedy to those who feel and a comedy to those who think." In that moment I quipped about me being the feeler and my husband being the thinker. I count on my husband's humour to put things in perspective and this equates to less tragic thinking.

Are you a feeler or a thinker? Who in your life is able to see life as a comedy? What can you learn from them and take with you as you move forward?

The Creative

Irene Mavis Voyatzis (1928-2019)

"She loved to pen witty poems for friends' milestones (as well as rhyming guidelines for cottage bathroom protocol), showcasing her humour and intellect. Every project, whether creative or compulsory, became an imaginative labour of love."

Among many other artistic talents, alongside middle school teaching, Irene was known for her *"clever couplet writing."* She was born in Scotland and raised by her grandmother. Couplet writing took root in Scotland with the penning of "The Brus" by John Barbour. This is a wonderful reminder that our own brand of humour and the way it is expressed can find its roots in our culture. I would love to know if Irene wrote couplets as a child alongside her grandmother. I can imagine them taking turns reading their finished work aloud to each other with a lovely Scottish lilt full of dramatic oral and facial expression.

A friend of ours posted a love letter in his bathroom that he wrote to a girl in his Grade 4 class. It deepened my appreciation for him, especially his ability to laugh at himself even after our good-natured ribbing. I've always felt that I can express myself far better with my writing (or a mixed cassette tape) than with spoken words, so I'm grateful to learn that Irene made her mark with her informal written offerings.

What childhood influences come to play in your sense of humour? Can you see glimpses of the humour of your parents, grandparents or other family members in your sense of humour?

The Showboat

Roland Gosselin (1945-2019)

"He kept his colleagues at the Government of NWT on their toes by sporadically showing up for work as "Rolanda" wearing a black wig and tight blue dress with an augmented chest. He relished making his colleagues uncomfortable, but he enjoyed mortifying his daughters even more. At home he would put on his tighty-whitey shorts (no shirt), knee high black socks, black dress shoes, and tool belt, simply to mow the lawn or sweep the road."

At first glance, Roland's torture by embarrassment might seem cruel, but it was part of a loving parental strategy. He also taught his girls *"how to change the oil in a car, chop wood, cut down the perfect Christmas tree, cast a fishing line, swim, be a strong negotiator, unfreeze a pipe with a blow dryer, use an auger for ice fishing, install baby gates, pan for gold and...* [wait for it]... *laugh often and laugh at yourself."* I'm pretty sure this last lesson was high on Roland's list. If it's high on your list, it might be time to find yourself a pair of tighty-whiteys.

I remember the kids in my Grade 8 French class announcing loudly, "Tammy, your mom is outside... isn't that *your mom?*" Sure enough it was. She was mastering cross-over side steps between two towering oak trees while simultaneously pumping 2-lb dumbbells. In a head-to-toe peach track suit no less. I slunk under my desk and swore that if I had kids I would never do anything to embarrass them. But of course I do. I've come to realize I do it for the same reason a toddler acts out. Toddlers push and smack because they enjoy impacting their environment A swift response from their caregiver proves that they are seen. Our teenage boys are increasingly opting for time with friends over time with my husband and me. When they gasp "Mom!" I know they see me.

What can you do to make sure you are seen (even if it means making a scene)?

The Goofball

Michael Ennis (1942-2018)

"We will remember Michael for his unfailing sense of humour and ability to provoke a laugh (or groan) when he appeared wearing a silly hat chosen from his special collection."

Michael's life was dedicated to public service culminating with his role as assistant deputy minister of the Ontario Ministry of Health. After retiring he volunteered for a lengthy list of health-related social programs. It notes that *"Those who had the honour of working alongside Michael will forever remember his ability to lead a team through calm or storm..."* What role did his *"unfailing sense of humour"* play in this gift of calm leadership? When we imagine Michael entering a room with a *"silly hat"* for the sake of making light, we know he didn't take himself too seriously. This must have played a role.

Doesn't everyone know a Michael? The groaners, the silly hat collection. This is a reminder that intent is king. Regardless of whether or not we have humour that resonates with those around us, being playful and putting yourself out there is the most important ingredient. We know Michael's family agrees, because they made a point of including this in his obituary.

What goofy stunts do you pull to garner a laugh? Can you pull out any new tricks for the remainder of the ride?

The Accidental Comedian

Dr. Aubrey Groll (1934-2018)

"His characteristic lightness, 'horsey-rides,' silly songs, and famous malapropisms are the stuff of family lore."

I keep a dictionary nearby when I read the obits. Some pretty smart people write these life stories and often pull out their vocabulary big guns. It turns out a malapropism is "the mistaken use of a word in place of a similar-sounding one, often with an unintentionally amusing effect." Aubrey was the recipient of several prestigious professional awards for his practice and teaching as a gastroenterologist. He was well-known to be a compassionate physician who listened carefully and showed great empathy, often sharing his emotions with patients and families at difficult times. In short, he was willing and able to be human with others in all situations. That he was playful and willing to be the brunt of teasing for using the wrong word here and there is no surprise.

Malapropisms are my brand of humour as well. It wasn't until a Grade 4 trip to the zoo that I learned "fairy dogs" were in fact "prairie dogs" thanks to ridicule from 20-plus nine-year-olds. In university I handed in an essay using the word "little lone" multiple times in place of "let alone." Then there's Kenny Rogers and his "400 children and a crop in the field" that I have only very recently sorted out as being "four hungry children." When I accept that imperfection is endearing, and that unintentional laughs still count, I can own this.

> *Got any favourite malapropisms? Can you laugh at yourself to show others — and yourself — that you don't take yourself too seriously?*

The Eternal Kid

Maurice Henry Lecorney Pryce (1913-2003)

"He always kept a boyish liking for silly games, from elaborate sandcastles on the beach to noisy card games on the living room floor."

This "boyish" side of Maurice is particularly poignant upon learning that he left an indelible mark in the international realm of theoretical physics. As noted in his obituary *"he elucidated in detail the interaction between the magnetic electrons and the lattice (the crystal field), the effective lattice dynamics (the Jahn-Teller effect) and interaction with the nucleus (hyperfine structure)."* As important as I know these contributions to science must be, the part that I hold on to tightest is that he still made space for silly. That is one smart man.

My Dad died recently. He was a clever man who contributed to the field of pediatric radiology as an academic, professor and practitioner. What I appreciate most is his ability to be an unabashed goof. He had a facial expression for every occasion (I'm talking full facial contortion). He was known to hang a full moon to lighten the mood when saying good-bye, and he even made me a three-generation family tree with photographs of our "moons" in his final days. He taught me how to make armpit farts. I loved him most when he was unhinged and present.

I will take credit for the "full moon" at his informal ocean-side memorial service.

Are you able to access your inner kid? If not, what can you do to find it?

The Life of the Party

John (Jack) Edwin Lang (1914-1999)

*"Dad worked for 13 years as a milkman for Dairyland.
He made home deliveries in West Point Grey [Vancouver].
Because of his seniority, he drove one of Dairyland's first
two milk trucks. One of my favourite stories from this time
was when one of the families on his route bought a new
piano. For some reason they were up at 5 a.m. when dad
came by to deliver the milk. They invited him in to try the
new piano. Well one thing led to another and pretty soon
the party was underway. As the morning progressed, others
on the milk route awoke to find their milk hadn't been
delivered. Looking down the street they saw the milk truck
parked in the middle of the block. People began to wander
down with their empty bottles, tokens and coins. These they
exchanged for their allotted new full bottles of milk. Upon
leaving the truck they could hear the piano playing and
voices singing. So, they took their bottles of milk home to the*

ice box where they exchanged them for cases of beer, and headed back to the party. By 1 p.m. nobody cared if the new piano was in or out of tune — the party was in full swing. By 3 p.m. the milk truck had failed to return to the yard. By 5 p.m. one of the office staff came out to see what had happened to the truck and driver. Nobody had called in to report not receiving their milk. The truck was found in the middle of the block, where it had been since 5 a.m. It was in perfect order: with full bottles all exchanged for empties all neatly stacked in the appropriate cartons; all the tokens and change were in the tray. Each person had taken only what he or she was entitled to and had paid honestly for what was taken. The keys were still in the ignition. The party was still going strong, for by now the whole neighbourhood had joined in."

When Jack left Dairyland in the late 1940s to pursue a career as a writer, the customers on his milk route threw him a farewell party. The event made the *Vancouver Sun* newspaper, complete with picture and the headline "The Most Popular Milk Man in Town." His daughter who wrote his obituary notes *"It was fun growing up as Jack Lang's daughter."* She adds that children got to stay up extra late when Jack would come to visit and they would be enthralled for hours with jokes, stories and that same old magic coin trick. *"We laughed and laughed until the tears rolled down our cheeks, then we laughed some more."* She goes on to paint a picture of the adults gathering around to laugh at the kids laughing.

Few of us are natural-born entertainers like Jack Lang, but we can enjoy the company of people who are. A 2017 study published in the *Journal of Neuroscience* demonstrated that contagious social laughter was found to stimulate endorphin release in the thalamus, caudate nucleus, and anterior insula. Long before modern brain-imaging technologies proved that laughter is contagious, American psychologist and philosopher, William James, observed, "We don't laugh because we're happy, we're happy because we laugh." So even if we see something on our phones that we think is hilarious, unless we LOL (laugh out loud) something important is lost. We need the type of infectious laughter that grows wildly out of control when it is shared with another person. In short, we need the Jack Langs and we need each other.

Will you give yourself permission to stray from your routine the next time a character like Jack Lang captures your curiosity? How could you be the person who starts the party and captivates others?

The Good-Natured Nut

Doris Mary Ross Sturdee (1923-2017)

"As nearly as can be determined, not once in her life did she answer the telephone with a conventional 'Hello?' Instead, she would pick up the handset and emit some mystery phrase. 'What's it to ya?' she would growl. Or 'Gimme some o' that,' or 'Boo!'"

I wonder if Doris' grandkids ever rang her up solely for the entertainment of her greeting. I would have. Her unconventional telephone greetings are infinitely more welcoming than the dreaded "I haven't heard from you in awhile." Nothing kills a conversation as quickly as guilt. And nothing brings one to life like offbeat humour. If Doris answered, you knew the conversation would be anything but boring.

I long for the days when everyone had a land line, almost everyone listed their phone number and people didn't answer the phone with cautious scrutiny. In our case we don't even answer the phone. Come to think of it, I don't even know why we have a land line. But now that Doris has put a twist on the classic phone greeting, I'll be happy to pick up the phone next time it rings. And maybe the next time I answer the phone the telemarketer will hang up on me.

What new twist can you bring to a mundane task? What good-natured surprise can you spring to signal a break from the ordinary?

Honouring others-that-mother

MAY

Mother's Day is the single busiest day of the year for restaurants. Waffles in bed, hand-picked flowers, and multi-colour homemade cards are also classic ways to mark the day that celebrates moms. Who else makes a bigger difference in the early lives of children?

Of course there also is Father's Day and the lesser-known Grandparent's Day, but what about the aunts, uncles, and countless other adults who make the lives of young people better? Those of us who are parents know we can't do it alone. We want our kids to forge relationships with other trusted adults to turn to for advice, mentorship and perspective. Queue the others-that-mother; the influential women and men who contribute to the act of "mothering" defined as "bringing up a child with care and affection." Kids value these others-that-mother, and their parents value them too.

According to the 2016 Canadian census, 51.1 percent of couples have one or more kids. That means nearly half of Canadian couples do *not* have any children. Add to that number the women and men without children who are not part of couple, and you are looking at a significant number of not-parents. But this doesn't mean they can't play a pivotal role in the life of a young person. In fact, they likely have greater reserves of patience and creativity than those of us who do have kids.

Many extended families in Canada, ours included, are spread out geographically. My husband and I recognize the importance of adults that our kids can go to when neither of us will cut it, and *we* want to be a go-to for youth in our community. But you have to earn that role, and the obituaries offer lessons on how to do that.

What type of magic do these others-that-mother wield that make them a go-to for young people? Here are ten with a lesson to share.

Naughty and loving aunt

Catherine Doherty (1956-2019)

> *"Catherine's true joy was her life with Peter and the dogs, and being the naughty, and incredibly loving, aunt to her nieces and nephews. Nothing secretly pleased her more than being mistaken for their grandmother. In return, they showered her with love and support, particularly during the difficult final days."*

If there is one word I would want my nieces and nephews to use to describe me, it's "naughty." ("Loving" is a close second). Naughty suggests fantastically playful. Unconfined by convention. A safe haven where you can be called out, but not condemned. Aunts are in a unique position to play a role akin to friend, but with more years of insight and a deeply rooted familial investment.

Our boys have kick-butt aunts. With the geographical spread of our family, sometimes I feel the need to flirt with the role of naughty aunt in my interactions with them. It never goes well. I am quickly reminded that structure and consistency are cornerstones in parenting how-to books, and for good reason. Most actions that bring awe to an aunt are embarrassing when performed by Mom. The aunts (and uncles) have a corner on "naughty." Catherine finessed naughty and loving, and her nieces and nephews adored her for it.

How do you want to be remembered by the kids (that aren't yours) in your life? What need are you in a unique position to fill for a young person?

Foster-sister

Erie. M. Tudhope (1921-2020)

"At war's end, she took her 12-year-old stepbrother, Harry, under her wing. Harry, a paraplegic survivor of polio, had also lost his mother while in hospital and was in need of a strong, loving hand. Erie's nurturing instinct prevailed."

Erie was five years old when her mother died. This is when Erie *"began to develop an empathy for all living things, especially animals and the emotionally and physically challenged, that would be a hallmark of her life."*

A blind date while she was working for an investment firm in Toronto led to Erie and Alan getting married in 1949. Soon their family grew to include three sons. Erie's stepbrother Harry eventually joined the family's home and he and his young friends *"brought an aura of the merry prankster to an otherwise conventional suburban life."* Neighbours, children, aunts without families and a wide girth of friends and family were welcome to share a meal and a drink in the loving and inclusive home that

Erie created. A home that *"took on the quality of a community centre."*

Erie took Harry under her wing in extenuating circumstances. She was a young, single woman finding her way in the aftermath of the Second World War. She didn't have the support of a mother that most young adults rely on when they launch into life. Yet, she provided a safe haven for Harry then, and again later while nurturing her young family. Part of Erie's legacy lies in the lens with which her now-adult sons fondly recall the presence of Harry in their childhood home. She fostered Harry and her sons foster a strong appreciation for the value of a loving and inclusive home.

My grandfather was delivered to Reedham Orphanage in Surrey, England when he was five years old. After his parents died he was passed between his aunts until they could no longer shoulder the added financial burden. I deeply wish there had been an Erie in his life to welcome him into her family when he was sent on his way from Reedham at the age of sixteen. Fortunately he found his nurturer a decade later when he married my grandmother who was five years his senior and a seasoned mother hen to six brothers.

Is there someone in your life who might need your wing? Can you see how this person may add to the richness of life, in the way Erie's stepbrother did?

Shepherding aunt

Lynn Ann Stewart (1955-2019)

*"Lynn's nieces and nephews will remember her frequent
visits to the island where they had to account for the
plans they were making for their future. Advice on how to
achieve their goals followed — in detail. All done out of the
formidable love she had for each of them, combined with a
desire to stay connected with her family and with the greater
community of Murray Harbour."*

The offerings of aunts extends beyond lawless visits complete
with the contraband of childhood — candy, pop, horror movies
and too-late bedtimes. Lynn meant business and her nieces
and nephews were beneficiaries of her guidance. I picture Lynn
peering over reading glasses perched on the end of her nose to
create an atmosphere of serious dignity and then smiling fondly
as her nieces and nephews flesh out their vision of their future
selves.

I would like to make a point of asking the young people in my life more questions about their ideas around education, career and other big life decisions. When they ask for advice I will remember Lynn and won't hold back.

What things do you feel qualified to give advice to young people about? Sometimes the best way to support someone else is to ask questions and listen. What questions can you ask?

The Renaissance Uncle

Paul Joshron Portnuff (1932-2010)

"Paul took it upon himself to share his knowledge and love of all things musical with his nephews, whom he loved, respected and treated as his own children."

Paul's lifelong love of piano, opera and classical music began at age three. His love for the arts remained a constant during and after pursuing medicine followed by graduate studies in pathology. He awakened an appreciation for opera and classical music in others — from family members to the employees of local music stores — by virtue of his infectious enthusiasm. He was an uncle that *"freely gave advice, whether solicited or unsolicited"* and he was *"the family source of knowledge on topics as diverse as opera, science fiction, historical fiction, Latin, 20th century art, and movies ranging from Kurosawa to John Carpenter to Pixar cartoons."* If all this wasn't enough, he was also a talented chef, photographer, story-teller and fashion maven.

Did life without children of his own enable Paul to take bigger bites out of life? Did his freedom from familial responsibility create space for visits to the galleries, plays and symphony performances that fuelled his knowledge? These nephews were privy to a rich perspective that only a Renaissance uncle like Paul could provide.

Although we've made it to a small handful of music festivals and concerts since our boys were born, the only musical performances we write with pen on our calendar are those of the high school band. I like to tell myself that I would be a riveting musical diva if I didn't have children.

What knowledge have you socked away that might fuel the interest of another person? Is there someone you know with a wealth of knowledge that might share it with you?

Honorary 'Auntie'

Margaret Elizabeth Moffat (1916-2018)

"After losing her parents as a child, Margaret was adopted by close friends of her parents, Dr. and Mrs. Ashley Fife of Fort William. In her early teens, Margaret and her 'Auntie' travelled the world by ship, visiting such places as Hawaii and Australia. In addition, they travelled to Italy including an audience with the Pope and to England where they had tea at Buckingham Palace."

Margaret lived to be a great-great-grandma to four children. As a close friend of her parents, her "Auntie" (Mrs. Fife) must have been able to regale Margaret with stories about the inner beauty of her mother and relay how deeply her parents adored her. This connection to her mother, through "Auntie," must have been especially comforting when Margaret became a mother herself. Would Margaret have been afforded the same travel opportunities and encounters with her parents as the youngest of four children? Despite a tragic loss early in life, "Auntie" gave young Margaret the gift of many life experiences, all made more incredible knowing this was in the early 1930s.

Most of us with young kids have a plan for the unthinkable — leaving them behind in the world without us. Dr. and Mrs. Fife stepped up to the parenting plate and provided astounding, worldly experiences to Margaret. I find it comforting to imagine our boys enveloped in a life full of love and experience in the event we leave them too soon.

Were there others-that-mother in your childhood that expanded your world or your thinking? How can you expand the world or thinking of a child you know?

Open new worlds

Eileen Mary Hawryliw (1926-2018)

"She loved to recall her elementary-class trip to a Japanese restaurant to watch and then sample the quick frying of succulent chicken livers, or the rehearsing and travelling with her young students to Prince Albert for the local TV station's Amateur Hour...Field trips, spontaneous learning tangents, and, a friendly disregard for authority characterized her inimitable, enriched teaching style..."

By the age of 19, Eileen was teaching Grades 1 and 2 in small Saskatchewan farming communities. Her trips to Prince Albert required travelling more than 100 kilometres and likely a battery of logistics including permission slips and a big orange school bus. Did she take a child on the adventure even if their unsigned permission slip was found balled up in a coat pocket, inventing the saying "Act now. Apologize later"? Did her students living on poultry farms fry a chicken liver in a sizzling fry pan to share the experience with their parents? As adults do these former students now point out the places they visited with "Mrs. Hawryliw" to their own children, or stop to re-live and share the experience?

In her very first year of teaching, our high school English teacher spearheaded a student trip to New York City. She adores contemporary art, Broadway theatre and eccentric fashion, and she wanted us to experience *all* of it. Twenty of us fund-raised for an entire year and followed her onto that airplane during spring break 1987. Most of us are still in touch with her on Facebook, and thirty years later she is still nudging us out of our comfort zones with her poignant questions. When I took one of our boys to NYC we retraced the steps of this trip together and the breadth of the impact of her gift became clear.

How can you awaken the senses and curiosity of others to captivate their interest in a new experience?

Larger than life role model

George S.B. Moad (1946-2019)

"George was the driving force behind the 10th Toronto Cub Pack in the late 70s/early 80s. As the *Akela, his larger than life personality brought an immense sense of energy and excitement to the boys and leadership team, attracting them from throughout the neighbourhood. The pack was one of the strongest in the entire region. Monday night meetings, special outings and weekend camping trips were infused with his combination of fun-loving joie-de-vivre, no-nonsense drive to do things well, and great humour. He helped shape the lives of hundreds of boys and many still talk fondly about this big figure from these seminal growing-up years."

George and his wife Louise didn't have kids of their own. Instead George devoted himself to the young people in their community; teaching them new things, giving them experiences and ensuring they felt valued. To measure the spin-off of George's impact begin with "hundreds" and start multiplying.

The two non-family people that most significantly influenced my life are oblivious to their impact on me. One was a Grade 5 substitute teacher who told me that I would be a "great writer one day." I held that close when a first-year journalism professor told me I was "illiterate." The other was a woman I volunteered with at United Way. She was everything I wanted to be; smart, centred, running her own communications business and living a groovy urban social life. She spent time with me, lunched with me, invited me into her home and believed in me. And so I started to believe in me too.

> *What personality trait do you have that young people would be drawn to or learn from? Who influenced your childhood that you still have time to thank?*

*An Akela is a symbol of wisdom, authority, and leadership and refers to someone who acts as a leader to the Scout.

Enabling aunts and uncles

Dr. Margaret Jansen (1924–2018)

"Margaret was raised in Three Hills, Alberta on a homestead farm and attended a one-room schoolhouse. Her many aunts and uncle in Toronto enabled her to attend the University of Toronto and she graduated from the Faculty of Medicine in 1949. She spent her entire working life at Queen St. Mental Health Centre caring for outpatients."

Medical school might not have been possible for Margaret without the support of her aunts and uncle. She has payed this forward to the next generation. It notes at the end of her obituary that *"Because education was so important in her life, she funded the education of many in her extended family and beyond."* One will never be able to measure the ripple effect of the support provided by Margaret that started with her aunts and uncle.

I have an aunt who helped me early in life. I was 18, with no place to live when I arrived in Ottawa to start university. She showed me around the city, had me over for meals, lent me a bed for the oversized closet I rented and threw away my ripped jeans (I've only recently let go of the last one). She didn't hover, but I knew that she had my back and was just a phone call away. It was a tremendous support.

What can you do for the young people in your life to create a ripple effect?

Grampy Sherman

John Sherman Bleakney (1928-2019)

"...the grandkids have memories of him building a big painted school bus for them out of appliance boxes, making a kid-size tin-man outfit to dress up in after they and Grampy had watched the Wizard of Oz, devising an elaborate treasure hunt for pirate gold on a Nova Scotia beach (maybe a little too realistic!), laughing uproariously at Grampy's magic tricks, and wading in tide pools to collect sea life that they then marvelled at through Grampy's very cool dissecting microscope. Grampy Sherman remained a kid at heart and a great jokester throughout his life, and his grandkids brought out the best of this in him."

Sherman and Nancy were long-time empty-nesters in Nova Scotia who looked forward to yearly visits from their five grandchildren. It goes without saying that Grampy-time is remembered fondly and vividly. We can assume Grampy Sherman will continue to live on not only in stories, but in the *joie de vivre* his grandkids will bring to the young people in their lives when they become adults.

I have been taking notes for years as we watch our neighbours play host to their grandkids. Every Christmas they prepare for the stream of loyal visitors by creating a skating rink and toboggan run on their property. A crackling fire pit surrounded by benches plays host to marshmallow roasters. Spotlights dot the spiderweb of extension cords and light up laughing kids in bulky snowsuits. What could make a young person feel more important than having an entire winter playground created for the sole purpose of their enjoyment?

> *How do you let the kids in your life know they matter? You don't need to make buses out of boxes or create a skating rink to show your love. (Although that is pretty cool.)*

Opinion generator

Martha Bernice Home Currie (1925-2019)

"She was immensely proud of her family, doted on her grandsons, loved art and couldn't stand Trump."

Martha spoke her mind on the things that mattered to her, and we know her family took note because they included it in her obituary. Her strongly voiced admiration and unabashedly expressed distaste prove she was discerning. She was neither a Pollyanna nor a curmudgeon (although curmudgeons do have their own special charm).

No matter how hard we try to give our kids both sides of a story to enable them to formulate their own viewpoints, they are tainted by our biases. At least they were until they became teens; now they are often contrary to arouse a good debate. It took years for me to stop fretting about the antiquated opinions expressed by extended family members when our kids were in earshot. I've come to embrace their tirades as fodder for thought and conversation.

> *What strongly held opinion can you share with others to get them thinking? Letting others know you value their opinions — even if they don't align with your own — will set the stage for a great conversation and learning on both sides.*

Secrets to being likeable

JUNE

People spill out of their homes in June. Suddenly streets are dotted with kids on bikes, retired neighbours plant themselves in gardens under wide brim hats and people catch up on a winter's worth of gossip across lawns and over fences.

Most of us become more social as spring unfolds and summer finally arrives. June has the longest days of the year. People make plans to see faraway family and friends as kids count down the last days of the school year. It's a month to put our best social foot forward and enjoy the company of others. But what about *our role* in being good company? How can *we* be the person that others want to sit beside?

The obituaries are chock-full of references to the thing (or things) that made a person easy to love and hard to lose. When an entire lifetime is distilled to an average of 500 words, we know each word was carefully considered. I often think of obituaries as the handbook on "How to be Likeable."

My sister is a pediatrician who provides health care to more than 6,000 children. She uses the analogy of a diamond to describe children and our influence on them as parents. "You can polish them to make them shine brighter, but each of their unique angles and edges are already formed when they first land in your arms."

What makes each of us likeable is as unique as a diamond. We need the people who forget birthdays (but happily put out an extra dinner plate for a stranger) and the people who are scrooges over the holidays (but turn a blind eye when kids track mud into their kitchen). The following ten lessons from the obituaries on how to be likeable have inspired me to polish some of my angles and edges.

Don't get teed off, just get to tee off in time

James Gordon Cook (1926-2019)

"Mom had a temper, Dad did not. Unless you broke the one simple rule: the car must be home by 5:30 am on weekends so he wouldn't be late for his standard 6:30 am tee time at Summit. On occasion, one or more of the three reprobates would arrive home with minutes to spare to find Dad, resplendent in his Herb Tarlek inspired golf slacks, waiting anxiously at the end of the driveway. "Put it in park and get out! A man of very few words indeed."

Even though Gord loved to golf, it's pretty obvious that Marian, his wife of 60 years, the "three reprobates" (his sons) and his posse of six grandchildren were valued above all else. This is a man who sat on the sidelines watching his boys play sports and *"never once shouted at a referee, umpire or coach..."* He kept a cool head at home, by swinging madly on the greens.

When our kids were little I'd spread out on the floor to play with them. We'd leave paint footprints across the carpet, eat meals under the table and stop to examine every bug on neighbourhood walks.

By the time they turned 13 my patience had run dry. Today I bark at them, nag regularly, and some days have to give myself time outs. Recently my husband asked me, "How do you want them to remember you?" Gulp. I had fooled myself into thinking that the early years were akin to compounding interest: I thought all my deposits were gaining interest, ready to be pulled out by the handful at a date to be determined. The question from the man who drags all the mattresses into the living room for family movie night delivered a welcome reality check. Apparently recent memory pulls rank, leaving most of us with a smattering of the very best (and worst) memories to draw from our distant past.

So while my "fun Dad" husband builds up his stock options faster than our 15-year-old's feet are growing, I'm left sitting on pocket change. Cue Gord and his timely advice for parenting teenagers. It turns out my best parenting moments may be yet to come.

Are there things that tee you off that you could shrug off instead? (Not all of them, just a few.)

Laugh at yourself often

Shirley Chavarie (1935-2014)

"If you are reading this, I have passed my 'best before' date."

The beauty of the selfie-obit is that you get to take a jab at yourself. Self-effacing humour after you have died is a whole other level of good humour. Shirley dedicates two sentences of her eight-sentence obituary to thanking each of her children for their unique contribution to her full and happy life. *"...Jan, my no nonsense advisor and mentor; Kit, my health and reality checker; Gaylin for crossword brain food and jokes; Lee, my daily caller and locksmith. They should all get Olympic gold medals for geriatric care."* I can imagine Shirley standing in a doorway, turning away to leave for her next chapter saying "It's been a slice folks, but now I have to go". There is no drama, just gratitude and a lightness that sets the tone for how she wants others to carry on in her absence.

I spend a fair bit of time alone during the day because I work from home. I started to talk to myself long ago, but thanks to Shirley now I laugh at myself too. If the release of stress hormones isn't enough to convince you of the value of laughter, I just read a university-endorsed study that reports we burn 50 calories in 10-15 minutes of laughter.

What moments slip past you uneventfully that you could choose to laugh at? What heavy-hearted event can you find lightness in and in doing so accept the size of your grief is not a measure of how much you care?

Be open to having fun

Lorna Leslie Ellison (1914-2018)

*"They must have called one hell of a party in heaven for
Lorna to decide to leave us on Sunday, February 4, 2018."*

Can you picture Lorna at the head of the table cracking jokes
and slapping her knee with a signature belly laugh? I can too,
but as we read on we see more. *"Parties, big and small, family
dinners at Wendy's, quiet conversations with family or friends, the
anticipation of a new great-grandchild — this was the stuff that
brought happiness to the last quarter century of Lorna's 103-year
journey."* It didn't matter to Lorna if she was at a fancy soiree or
a burger joint, as long as she was with people she cared about.
She enjoyed these moments, and gave others the opportunity to
enjoy her, because she said "yes" and showed up.

The older I get the more I like to stay home. I have a long list of
excuses stockpiled for the last-minute bail on almost anything
social. But I want to be remembered the way Lorna is, as "a

friend, confident, guide and supporter to her friends and family"
until the end.

> *Can you say "yes" the next time an opportunity lands in your lap about which you are lukewarm?*

Draw others in with your enthusiasm

Joan Martin Waterous (d. 2015)

> *"She taught us all how to drive, how to revive pre-loved furniture, that good manners matter more than money, that ice cream is a food group, and that generosity is its own reward."*

I love the randomness of this list. This isn't a checklist from a parenting book. These lessons passed on by Joan are a love note from a parent who let life unfurl on its own time, sopping up opportunities to share, and infusing experiences with her enthusiasm. Because one of her children wrote it, we know this list represents offerings from Joan that were remembered and are still deeply valued by her now-adult children.

When my mom saw the "for sale" sign tacked to an antiquated boat in the back lane she shrieked "Tammy!" and grabbed my arm. Soon the 14-foot 1960s boat with a temperamental engine was docked on the Red River steps from my high school. I can count on one hand the number of times the boat left the dock, but it played host to many sleepovers. Mom would greet me after school on Fridays with "let's get [Big] Gulps" and we'd head to the boat. We pulled the back-to-back narrow seats into "beds," talked into the wee hours of the night and invented contraptions for a midnight pee. This enthusiastic spontaneity was a thread that ran through my childhood, be it a game of Rummy Cubes on the stairs of the Saint Boniface Cathedral at sunset, or a drive-thru for a burger prompted by a late-night TV commercial. I was drawn into the strong current of her enthusiasm, and over time my tendency towards predictability gave way to a love for launching into to the unknown which has served me well in life. Today routine is a necessary part of our overbooked life, but when I tap into the enthusiasm and spontaneity modelled by my mom, the most incredible moments unfurl with my boys.

How can you draw others in and share what you are enthusiastic about? How can you support and widen the circle of enthusiasm-generators around your children so that what they become passionate about knows no bounds?

Roll with it when sh*t doesn't go as planned

Sascha Armour (1930-2017)

"While preparing sit-down Christmas dinners often of 20 or more, many a turkey caught fire in their home much to the delight of grandchildren and the unease of guests."

In her school-age years Sascha travelled to many countries as part of a military family, including Great Britain where *"she carried a gas mask with her school lunch during the London blitz."* A long list of eye-opening life experiences early in life likely contributed to Sascha's ability to remain calm when things went sideways. As the mother of six children who made sure their home was *"an oasis for neighbourhood children,"* Sascha knew how to have fun *and* how to make fun. *"Her thematic birthday cakes, composed of sugar-coated tanks, liquorice cowboy wagons, and plastic farm animals, and her curated birthday outings to fire stations and maple syrup farms were legend."* But even when she went to great lengths to make life magic for her family, it's safe to say she found the fortitude to laugh when it didn't go as planned. In the words of Sascha, *"There are no rewards for pessimism."*

My mom often laments that it was a disaster when the power went out during a family reunion at her cottage. But playing Scrabble by candlelight and eating crackers with peanut butter for dinner is what made the reunion the one our kids remember most fondly.

How can you prepare yourself to laugh the next time something that matters to you goes sideways? Be easy on yourself and remember that Sascha had years of practice and many perspective-setting life experiences.

Tell stories about who you are, not what you do

Ruby Steiger (1921-2016)

"On her first night in Toronto, she went to the symphony in the pouring rain on a standing room only ticket, this anecdote so evocative of her adventurous spirit, joyousness in the most inclement of weather and passion for music."

As a young nurse Ruby moved from Yarmouth to Toronto to care for veterans returning from the Second World War. It was there she fell in love with an Austrian-born artist at the home of a friend during an afternoon salon where she played the piano. *"This dark romantic figure appeared at her door stoop the next day, a record under his arm, saying, 'This is how it should be played!'"* She married this man and together they grew a family who reaped the rewards of their shared love for, and talent in, music and the arts.

It's not our education, our job titles or who we rub elbows with that make others want to know us better. Sometimes a single story speaks volumes of our character and what we value enough to take risks for. Take some time to remember your defining moments. Share them. Invite others to share theirs.

Next time you meet someone can you try "what do you get up to when the rest of the world doesn't need you?" or "what is the scariest thing you have done for fun?" rather than "what do you do for a living?"

Strut the things that defy your stereotype

Johanna Helfinger (1930-2019)

"Her tastes were eclectic; she adored books on Charlemagne as well as Peanuts cartoons. She could recite lines from Shakespeare and Mel Brooks. She devoured scholarly works on the Middle Ages, but also loved Good Housekeeping and The People's Friend."

Daily life can be tedious, so we are intrigued by people who go against the grain. Johanna worked tirelessly in a chocolate factory while memorizing Latin declensions and persevering through Tacitus and Pliny. Good luck stereotyping that.

A good friend of ours is the Executive Director of *Kamloops Innovation*, a non-profit that champions tech start-ups in a myriad of creative ways. He and his family own *Freith Farm*, a 160-acre sheep and hay farm 40 minutes outside of Kamloops. He kicks off his weekends by reading the latest tech news through the eyes of his Ph.Ds in Artificial Intelligence and

Computational Neuroscience, and then heads to his fields to wield a 200-year-old approach to farming and animal rearing. This juxtaposition fascinates many people, including me.

What do you do that might surprise others? Can you tell others about the things that move you? You might be surprised by what is surprising about you.

Zig when they zag

Peter J. Austin-Smith (1932-2019)

"He once presented a conference paper on the migration patterns of Phoenicopterus ruber ornamentalis (aka plastic pink flamingoes) to a puzzled audience. He wrote and published serious reports and papers, but never took himself too seriously."

Anyone who attended Cornell University and taught Biology at Acadia University, as Peter did, has good reason to take themselves seriously. Peter also worked in the field as a wildlife biologist re-establishing bald eagles in Massachusetts and peregrine falcons in the upper Bay of Fundy, among other projects.

We can surmise that Peter poured countless hours into producing the academic papers he wrote and presented. With his vast knowledge, he could have spoken confidently on any number of topics, like the other distinguished presenters. Instead, Peter chose to offer a much-needed light-hearted laugh at a science-based conference. In doing so he revealed his lack of ego, and who doesn't like a smart guy without an ego? (Guess whose presentation folks remembered long after the conference?)

How can you lighten the mood by taking yourself less seriously?

Let others in on a little secret about yourself

Pearl Yvonne Cathcart (1929-2019)

"She had one unrealized dream — to be a journalist. On a recent move, her children discovered dozens of notebooks full of quotes and her thoughts on issues at the time."

Pearl was a devoted mother who made sure her kids ate three vegetables with dinner, but she was also a passionate learner who closely followed political and international affairs. Born in Barrie, Ontario in 1929 when its population was 7,000, Pearl's attentiveness to politics likely made her an outlier.

I wonder what she wrote in her notebooks about Newfoundland becoming Canada's 10th province in 1949, or changes to the Indian Act in 1960 that gave First Nations people the right to vote. Did she share what she learned with other at-home mothers over a cup of tea and delight in the conversation that followed, or did she hold what she knew close, yearning for others to open the door for a good debate? Did she tuck her spiral notebooks into the back of the kitchen junk drawer when she heard the front door open? Did she write after everyone went to bed under the light of the moon in the hallway? Pearl was humble and sincere in her thirst for information and love of knowledge. Her secret notebooks are a testimonial to this.

I write poetry through the eyes of my 14-year-old self. It's raw and sometimes uncomfortable for others to read, but it's a way to connect with young people and show them that this mother still has the ability to relate to life as a teen. Reading from my work is how I preface poetry writing workshops to create a safe space for others to write and, sometimes, share. I have come to realize that the sharing of secrets, like most human interactions, has to be reciprocal. I am a believer in the value of secrets when they are yours to share.

I'm not talking TMI (too much information) here. I'm talking about the small intimate details we stumble upon when we take the time to get to know others. We need to let people in — even if it's just a little at a time — if we want them to invest in a relationship with us.

How can you let others know that you provide a safe place for their secrets?

Imperfection is endearing

Doris Mary Ross Sturdee (1923-2017)

"She was a constant source of giddy, spontaneous humour to all who knew her, and yet she could not tell a conventional joke to save her life. That was fine, because her frequent failed attempts at joke-telling were vastly funnier than the jokes she was trying to tell."

"She wrote everything down and then lost track of her notes."

"She once spent an entire month wearing a strange pair of eyeglasses that, it would later turn out, she had salvaged from a parking lot."

I just can't get enough of the late Doris Mary Ross Sturdee. Tell me you wouldn't love to have her as a friend, or at least have her along for a night on the Las Vegas strip. Her self-effacing imperfection is endearing, but Doris also came through when she was needed. She is described as "*an unorthodox but diligent parent, the sort of mother who drove her children just about everywhere, often delivering them to the correct destination at the appointed time.*" It wasn't until I had read her obituary several times that I caught the word "often." Does this one word refer to the day the Ross Sturdee kids showed up on a doorstep with a carefully wrapped birthday gift only to be greeted by an exhausted mother with a mop in hand? Or the time they showed up for their piano recital at the wrong church and sat in empty pews until the clergy ushered them out? It's unlikely that Doris tried to be imperfect, but I'm going to guess she was exactly the type of person she wanted to be, and that others loved her for it.

Our house is almost always a mess. I stopped apologizing and making excuses long ago because I'm not sorry and my only excuse for the mess is that a clean house isn't important enough to me to take action. I've come to accept comments like "what a kid-friendly home!" and "I really feel like I can put my feet up here" as the compliments they are intended to be. I like to think I am lowering the bar for others so they can use the time they spend apologizing for the state of their house to talk about something more interesting.

What foibles and forgetfulness of your own can you choose to see as endearing?

A love letter to immigrants on Canada Day

JULY

None of the people featured in this chapter were born in Canada, but each in their own way has made Canada a better place.

They were born in different countries, yet a common thread runs through their obituaries. A deep appreciation is expressed for their resilience and determination.

I wanted the collection of obituary excerpts in this chapter to represent someone from each continent. But during my research I encountered huge gaps. Different cultures memorialize death in different ways. Many cultures do not acknowledge death with a written obituary, and cost and language are potential barriers to a published obituary.

I also discovered that trends in obituaries run alongside trends in demographics. For example, Canada became home to 39,636 Syrian refugees between November 2015 and December 2016, but I have yet to come across the obituary of someone who was born in Syria in a Canadian newspaper. This demographic, however, may make itself known in the obituaries in the future. In the years to come, I suspect we will hear more life stories of ingenuity, creativity, and yes — resilience and determination.

This chapter showcases the diversity of the skills, life experiences, and contributions of those who choose Canada as their home.

Gave money generously

Poul-Erik Skovsbo Hansen (1940-2019)

"A proud Dane, Poul immigrated to Canada at the young age of 21 with $50 and a dream. Speaking no English he struggled to be taken seriously as a tool and die maker and began sweeping the floors at a toy factory at night. A strong work ethic carried him far, and within a decade, he had built a successful multinational auto parts company."

In 2018, Poul and Susan Hansen made a gift of $5 million to help establish the Poul Hansen Family Centre for Depression at Toronto Western Hospital. Their daughter received care at this Hospital which brought their attention to the value of the care provided and the need for expanded services. Their contribution extends the reach of mental health care to thousands of patients across Ontario, improving access to leading psychiatrists and treatment for depression and mood disorders.

According to the 2010 *Canada Survey of Giving, Volunteering and Participating*, immigrants were about as likely to donate money as people born in Canada, but they contributed more on average each year ($554) than Canadian-born donors ($409). Some people think that immigrants are a drain on government-funded services and, in turn, us. We need to pull the plug on that thought. The number one reason immigrants donate is "to give back."

Can we shift our thinking to see each new immigrant to Canada as another pillar adding support to our foundation and making it stronger?

Quashed hatred and intolerance

George Brady (1928-2019)

"He was liberated from the Death March in January of 1945 and returned home to find out that he was the sole survivor of his family. George felt that he should not dwell on the past and chose to make a new life in Canada honouring the legacy of his parents."

George's early years are well-known through the book *Hana's Suitcase*, which follows George and his sister Hana's journey from their Czech home to Terezin and finally to Auschwitz where Hana died.

Hana's suitcase was found in Auschwitz after the war and it became part of a small collection of children's items on loan at the non-profit Tokyo Holocaust Education Centre. Children visiting the Centre noticed Hana's name written on it and had many questions about the girl who once carried the suitcase. Fumiko Ishioka, the director of the Centre, was able to trace the suitcase to George. His willingness to share the story of his wartime journey with Hana led to the book (printed in more than 40 languages), television documentaries, a stage play and a feature film. George and his daughter Lara toured the world talking to school kids about the evils of racism and hate.

Humans depend on personal stories to build understanding. Historical accounts told through numbers and geographic points alone do not engage us in the same way. Hana's story invites us to deeply relate to an unfathomable atrocity — the death of a million Jewish children. People like George who are willing to be vulnerable and share their personal story appeal to our empathy. Empathy has the power to create change. Many of us try to protect others by tucking our stories away. George shows us that some stories are meant to be shared.

Do you have a story to share that will build understanding for others?

Improved equal access to education

Aisha Tara Umar (1969-2019)

"She possessed a zest for life, with the finest blend of mischief and adventure, believing that things were put in front of us to grab hold of and experience. And she believed in the strength and power of a community, in all its diversity, and that together we could do anything; and often reminding us by saying 'We've got this....'"

Born in Lahone, Pakistan, Aisha immigrated to Canada with her parents as a child. She lived in Montreal, Calgary and Toronto and earned an MBA at Queen's University. She worked mostly at the executive level for several information technology firms including IBM, Microsoft and AT&T. Aisha also worked for the Office of the Lieutenant Governor of Ontario and *D2L (Desire to Learn). She died after a battle with cancer shortly after her 50th birthday. *"Her fiercest love of all was dedicated to her daughter Yasmin."*

As Technology Advisor to the Lieutenant Governor of Ontario, Aisha focused on leveraging technology to improve education for children. "Technology is the great equalizer," Aisha said in an interview with *Biot Canada Magazine* in 2010. "Education is not a privilege, it is a right in my books." She helped to get technology into fly-in indigenous camps in remote regions of Ontario, driven by her belief that people should be provided with the tools to learn in their own community rather than be uprooted and sent to a larger centre to learn far away from family and friends.

Many people immigrate to Canada to provide opportunity to their children. Is this what brought Aisha's parents to Canada? *Canadian Immigrant* magazine lists "access to education is a priority in Canada" as one of the biggest reasons people immigrate. Was Aisha inspired to make education accessible to others because of the sacrifices her parents made for her education? Aisha was a coveted IT expert who found a way to leverage her skills to improve access to education for kids at a geographical or economic disadvantage.

How can you leverage your skills and talent to further something that really matters to you?

* Desire to Learn harnesses technology to transform learning and believes that everyone should have access to the best possible learning opportunities.

Gave minorities strong voices

Irene Gunhild Olljum (1926-2019)

"A joyous and relatively carefree youth was interrupted by the Soviet invasion of Estonia in 1940. Being of Swedish descent, she and her family were able to be evacuated to Sweden in July 1944 before the Iron Curtain dropped. In Stockholm she met and married Estonian refugee Rudolf Olljum in May 1950, and together they immigrated to Canada in May 1951."

Irene was a pioneer as a female business manager of a North American car dealership in the 1950s. One of her proudest accomplishments was receiving the Certified Professional Accountant designation at the age of 89! She was honoured to receive the Gold Medal of the Royal Order of the Polar (Northern) Star for her volunteer work to preserve and advance Swedish language and culture in Canada. She was given the Estonian National Council Award for her volunteer work for the Estonian community in Vancouver.

According to a *Women of Influence* magazine article, women still hold only 17 percent of management positions in the Canadian car dealership industry. Irene helped pave the way for that 17 percent. But it's Irene's dedication to preserving and advancing the language and culture of her homeland that fills me with awe. I am proud that Canada is a mosaic where the heritage of those who call Canada home is celebrated. I also appreciate being reminded that as we move through life we can take something precious with us from one chapter to the next. Irene not only brought the language and culture of her birth country with her to Canada, she educated others about the importance of her culture and grew a community dedicated to its preservation.

> *What do you value about your culture that you can share with others and, in doing so, give it strength and build understanding? How can you help turn up the volume of the voices of minorities?*

Help feed others' dreams

Celestina Belluz (1922-2020)

"With Europe's economy in tatters following the wars,
Celestina and Gino decided to leave Italy, dreaming of
the prospect of an education and a better life for the
next generation....In Canada, Gino started working as a
carpenter and to earn extra money, Celestina turned their
home into a residence for boarders who had also recently
arrived from Italy."

As a child Celestina helped around the house and tended to her
family's farm —caring for pigs, planting the garden, cooking and
washing dishes. These early years of hard work led to Celestina's
legendary discipline. She and Gino were a dynamic team,
building a new life from scratch in Toronto's Italian community.

They raised two sons and eventually achieved the kind of
economic stability they immigrated to Canada hoping to find.
Their oldest son, Renzo, was called to the Bar as a member of

the Law Society of Ontario in 1975 and continues his practice as a partner in a law firm. Their second son, Paul, graduated with a degree in Industrial Engineering and worked in management for IBM-Canada in Ontario, and later for IBM-North America in New York State, until retirement.

Studies show that immigrants who are focused on building a better future for their children, like Celestina and Gino, set the bar high with their strong work ethic. This translates into higher expectations of academic success for their children. A 2019 Statistics Canada labour market study found that 43 per cent of the children of immigrants completed a university degree compared to 29 per cent of the children whose parents were born in Canada.

Celestina's contribution to her family's success in Canada is memorable. She worked long hours serving others and exemplified an astounding work ethic. Her sons reaped the rewards of her strong example.

The reverence that Celestina's children and five grandchildren hold for her cleverness, resourcefulness and hard work is obvious. And she must have been one heck of a cook because her obituary assures us that *"Above all, it's her cooking that her family will remember."* Saluti!

> *Who in your life contributed to where you are today? In what ways have you worked behind the scenes for family, friends or community?*

Put Canada in the international limelight

Dr. Rajat Kumar Bhaduri (1935-2019)

"Rajat joined the McMaster faculty in the Physics Department in 1968... His passion and curiosity for physics was a driving force for his many accomplishments. Over sixty years he worked in many areas including: nuclear, particle, condensed matter, chaos theory, connections between number theory and physics, quantum mechanics and supersymmetry, statistical mechanics, Bose-Einstein Condensates, and astrophysics (including black holes).

Rajat was born in Raipur, India. He was the youngest of nine children and had *"a carefree, loving childhood."* He earned BSc and MSc degrees from the University of Calcutta and then studied radio physics at the Atomic Energy Training School. He worked as a Research Assistant in Theoretical Physics at the Tata Institute of Fundamental Research before coming to McMaster University and completing his PhD in Physics in two years (usually a minimum four-year pursuit). After working at Oxford

University as a Research Assistant, Rajat joined the McMaster Physics Department in 1968. A gifted teacher and mentor to many PhD and MSc students, he was widely known for being generous with his time and hospitality. Colleagues and students alike were frequent guests for delicious dinner parties hosted with his loving wife Manju.

Professor Rajat Bhaduri's contribution to physics is recognized internationally. He published three books and approximately 200 scholarly papers. After retiring as a professor in 2000, Rajat continued publishing papers in theoretical physics until his last days.

I found an article printed in the *Toronto Star* (February 19, 2015) with the headline "Canadian Scientists take aim at Big Bang Theory." Dr. Rajat Bhaduri was one of these scientists, and he was 80 at the time. I'm proud that this incredibly smart, curious man who wasn't afraid to challenge convention called Canada home.

> *How can we acknowledge the genius of our colleagues and neighbours who chose Canada as home? What questions can we ask to learn from those who come to Canada later in life?*

Cultivated future chemists

Agripina Palade Iribarne (1922-2019)

*"A Doctor of Industrial Chemistry, for many years she was
Senior Tutor at the Department of Chemical Engineering
and Applied Chemistry of the University of Toronto as well
as lecturer at the University of Buenos Aires. Her research
led to numerous publications covering topics related to
analytical chemistry, electrochemistry, industrial hygiene,
heat and mass transfer and fluid dynamics. She was known
as a demanding but caring teacher to her many students."*

Agripina lost everything and rebuilt her life in a new country
with a new language at least twice. As a young woman she left
her homeland of Romania as a refugee and began her studies
in Berlin. When the Second World War erupted, Agripina fled
Berlin for Argentina. It was here she earned her doctorate at
the University of Buenos Aires, one of the largest universities in
Latin America and alma mater of four Nobel Prize winners.

When Agripina immigrated to Canada in 1966, she was one of the few women in the Chemical Engineering Department at the University of Toronto. Agripina's credentials would have made her a welcome addition to any university in the world, but she chose Canada. In doing so she bolstered the next generation of Canadian chemists and made inroads for future generations of female chemists. It's understandable that Agripina was demanding of her students because she demanded a great deal from herself as well.

Forty-six percent of all doctoral graduates in Canada received their training from an institution outside of Canada. When these graduates choose Canada as home they contribute to the education of future graduates at Canadian universities.

I am grateful to live in a country that can draw an academic of Agripina's calibre. After reading her obituary I find myself taking stock of what I love and value about living in Canada so that I consciously choose it rather than become complacent about my good fortune of being born here.

Why would you choose Canada as your home even if it chose you first?

Trained twice to become a doctor

Dagmar Vosu, M.D. (1917–2019)

"Born, raised and educated in Rekvere, Estonia, Dagmar got her medical degree from the University of Tartu during World War II. She practiced medicine in Estonia then Sweden before settling in Montreal. She raised two children while re-qualifying to work in Quebec."

While at McGill University Dagmar rode the ambulances on emergency calls and was profiled in the *Montreal Gazette* in 1952 as the "Petite Physician on Wheels." After rigorous re-training, including three months responding to ambulance calls, she went on to specialize in anaesthesia and spent most of her career at the Lachine General Hospital.

What is required of people like Dagmar who come to Canada as a practicing physician from another country? Provided their medical degree was earned at a university recognized by the Medical Council of Canada, they are invited to requalify by doing *all* of the following: 1.) Writing a national exam to assess their medical knowledge; 2.) Doing two years of postgraduate medical training to practice family medicine (four-to-five years for other specialties), and; 3.) Passing a national association-regulated exam. This entire process is dependent on securing one of the small number of residencies available to non-Canadians.

Soon after arriving in Canada with her husband in 1951, Dagmar responded to ambulance calls while pregnant. When asked by the Montreal Gazette if she was ever nervous responding to these emergencies she said, "Why, I've never been nervous in my life," and added that her ability to speak Estonian, German and Swedish, as well as English, came in handy when attending to calls.

There are 4.6 million Canadians aged 12 and older without a primary health care provider. A recent article from *The Hamilton Spectator* sums up the situation; "Canada is dangerously short on doctors - and isn't training enough new ones to close the gap. Doctors educated abroad are willing and able to help. Canada must welcome more of them."

Dagmar offers a wonderful lesson in putting your ego aside and doing what is required, even when you know you already have what it takes. Thanks to her tenacity she played a much-needed role in providing medical care to Canadians.

Is there red tape you can cut through with a dogged determination? What could you start today rather than waiting for circumstances to get easier?

Advocated for our environment

Professor George Alexandrowicz (1942-2019)

"George was born in Tehran, Iran in 1942 as a war refugee. He is a graduate of the University of Toronto, where he met his wife of 51 years, and Harvard Law School. He mentored and taught students in international law, land transactions, and wills and trusts at Queen's University Faculty of Law since 1967."

In a **Queen's Law** tribute to Professor George Alexandrowicz fellow faculty member John Claydon notes, "That decade [the 1970s] was the most critical for the development of international law in this country's history, and George was at the centre of it all." George was involved with the federal Department of Environment's preparations for the UN's first major conference on international environmental issues (1971), the Stockholm Conference (1972), and the Convention on the Law of the Sea Convention negotiations (1973-82). In the same *Queen's*

Law tribute, student Evis Alimehmeti addresses his mentor's contribution to the future generation of Canadian lawyers:

> *"All of us non-Canadian students made it through the program because of the fatherlike support of Professor Alexandrowicz. Every week he would stop by our grad room to ask how we were doing and how he could be of help. It was amazing how he could understand our worries and obstacles with no words being spoken. He and his dearest wife Toni opened the doors of their home to us. I chose to conduct more of my research at Queen's because it had people like him."*

By inviting law students into their home Professor Alexandrowicz and his wife supported them much like relatives would.

Many of us set personal boundaries that keep those with less power at an arm's length. We err on the side of formality for fear of being misunderstood. Add the simple fact that nurturing others above and beyond what is expected takes time. If we weren't confined by caution or a too-packed schedule we could do more to support others.

> *What can you do to support someone who is working tirelessly to reach their goals?*

Helped conquer cancer

Dr. Skaria Alexander (1938-2019)

"'Alex' was born in Kerala, India. He went to medical school in Ludhiana, India then specialized in radiation oncology in the UK. In 1973, he immigrated with his family to Saskatoon, where he practiced at the Saskatchewan Cancer Agency. In 1981, he moved to Victoria, to practice at the BC Cancer Agency at the Royal Jubilee Hospital, until his retirement in 2002."

After retirement Alex volunteered at the Island Prostate Centre and was part of a team that conducted Canada's largest prostate cancer prevention trial (2002-2010). If we were all passionate enough about our work to do it without pay (provided our living needs were met) we could continue to further advancements in our field even after retirement.

Can you think of a way to contribute to your life's work after the pay cheques stop?

You say it's your 'Birthday'

AUGUST

As I write this chapter a milestone birthday stares me down. In August I turn five-oh. Age is a means to neatly group humans for everything from soccer leagues and art workshops to movie theatre ticket prices. Moving into the 50+ age group feels like a seismic shift.

When someone notes an age in an obituary it denotes a remarkable feat. It says "not only did they do this, but can you believe they did it at *this* age!?" It's worth scanning obits for these numbers because they can deliver inspiration or plant a seed. I am not easily inspired. I haven't looked at any of these ten people and said to myself "I absolutely *need* to do that," although I am gobsmacked that *they* did it. I will admit though, they've inspired me to add a few things to my bucket list, like tackling some new social media apps and checking out jazz clubs in Montreal.

We pay attention to age milestones from the very start of a life; date of the first smile, the first tooth and the first steps. The handful of things that are inextricably tied to age continue; when you can legally drive a car, your first drink in a pub and the day you can start collecting old age security cheques. Of course we all have commitments and limitations that stand in the way of our plotting, but sometimes the only thing standing between us and what we want most is our own proviso.

What if we resolve to nudge our ordinary moments here and there so that our next milestone year brings a personal blaze of glory? Or, if you prefer to dabble in non-committal bliss like me, what can you add to your list of things to try?

Here, by decade, are ten people who tackled an unlikely achievement for their age, and a takeaway lesson for our own journey. It's never too early. It's never too late.

Note: The titles in this chapter reflect a soundtrack because music is right up there with obituaries on the list of things that feed my soul.

Teens   'Go Your Own Way'

Roderick James McLeod (1933-2019)

"At 17, he ran away to New York City (from Toronto) to hear jazz at the clubs on 52nd street, but being underage, could only listen at the door. He was fortunate enough to see most of the greats from Billie Holliday to Bird, and supported most of the locals as well..."

Unlike Roderick, many teens are content to be escorted by their hovering parents through the high school years. A smooth transition to adulthood awaits as their parents transport them and their belongings to university or college. Their suitcases are unpacked, debit cards loaded, and the fridge is stocked before the parents give them a teary wave goodbye. Roderick gave up the safety net to follow his relentless passion for jazz, the impetus for his early independence.

I left my home in Winnipeg two days after I turned 18 to study journalism at Carleton University in Ottawa. I landed without a place to live and ended up renting a room in a cock-eyed home with three second-year university students. All three of them were men. I had only lived in a home with a single mom and sisters. It turned out to be an outstanding first year away from home with many valuable life lessons. From there I launched, wiser for the experience and grateful that neither one of my parents interfered.

Can you think of a moment when you championed your own independence? Remember this moment when a young person you know busts a move in pursuit of their passion.

20s   'With My Own Two Hands'

Dieter Ernst Gollnow (1936-2019)

"After leaving East Berlin and arriving in Quebec City by ship at 20, Dieter embraced everything he could to become Canadian and create an incredible life for his family. As a tool and die maker, he started his first company National Trading and Manufacturing Ltd before his 25th birthday. Dieter built one of the first seatbelts in Canada and also held multiple patents."

I can imagine Dieter standing on the windswept upper deck squinting towards the Quebec City skyline as the ship took aim for port. His hand patting his chest pocket one last time to make sure his landing documents were ready to go. In the obituaries there is a strong representation of men who worked as tool and die makers in another country before building a successful company in Canada. When you couple the tenacity required to work long, physically intensive days as a tool and die maker with the guts required to start a new life overseas, it stands to reason success was in their cards. In the 1980s Dieter became involved in the glass industry and was a champion of energy-conserving glass as a critical tool towards addressing global warming. Even after realizing his dream of financial success in Canada, he continued to think innovatively and take financial risks. His earth-friendly glass will continue to grace landmark buildings in Toronto such as Harbourfront Centre, Trillium Hospital and Durham College.

Many Canadians have a parent who immigrated to this country to build a better life for their family (or family-to-be). A whopping 39.4 percent of Canadians were either born outside of Canada, or have at least one parent who was born outside of Canada. When I read the obituary of a man like Dieter who launched into the unknown at such a young age, it reminds me that opportunities exist beyond the boundaries of our country. Travel to faraway places has never been easier. But Dieter also reminds me we can be thirsty for innovation and take entrepreneurial risks in the country I was born in. Canada is still a land of opportunity where innovation and entrepreneurial spirit are supported.

If you imagine your homeland through the eyes of the 20-year-old Dieter, does it change how you embrace it? Do you see the opportunity for innovation that he saw?

30s   'Shake Up the Neighbourhood'

Ilse Gordon (1941-2016)

"Ilse the bohemian seeker found her true calling with her first Tai Chi class. Her tai chi sword glinting in the sunlight over the chain link fences set her apart from the other 1970s suburban Oakville housewives and firmly on a path of lifelong learning and wellness."

Ilse's individuality shone early: *"As a teenager, she dyed her hair mauve (to match her Vespa) and regularly slipped out of her bedroom window to become a jitterbug champion in the 1950s small town of Wetzlar."*

Tai chi arrived in Canada in 1970, just five years before Ilse. She helped give rise to the practice which grew to 15,000 people strong in Canada by 2007. Because Ilse was unabashed about going against the grain of suburbia to follow her calling, she inspired countless people spanning four continents to "*transform their lives, overcome adversity and become their best selves.*"

The glinting tai chi sword that Ilse held high when she arrived in Canada enabled her to cut a wide swath for the many people who continue to reap the rewards of her trailblazing in Tai Chi, Chi Kung, yoga and meditation.

I'm learning that pressure to "keep up with the Joneses" or to conform to a certain way of living is a self-imposed fallacy. We can't possibly be held accountable for following rules if we aren't playing the game. I feel confident that Ilse was adored for her individuality, even if tongues wagged in suburbia when she first held high her glinting sword. If there were outliers they were either envious or intimidated.

> *What is your version of a "sword that glints over suburbia"?*

40s   'My Heart Has a Mind of its Own'

Andrew Bentham Batten (1963-2019)

Although Andrew studied and practised law for several years, he found his true calling as a high school teacher, after receiving his Bachelor of Education at York University in 2002.

Andrew was on the cusp of 40 when he started his teaching career. His "*mind and imagination knew no limits*" and his fearlessness with changing career gears appears to be no exception. Andrew immersed himself in acting and writing plays, his "*other two passions,*" and he contributed his talents in both realms to the Toronto theatre scene. He leveraged this artistic talent to engage his students. Andrew was often "*approached by former students who told him how much he had changed their lives for the better. Andrew was the teacher you always wished you had.*"

Many people make superficial changes in their forties, what some call a "midlife crisis." This is different. Andrew shows us that it's never too late to realign our life with our purpose and passions.

"One former student recently wrote on Andrew's Facebook page, 'Andrew was that special kind of teacher who really, deeply cared. He inspired me enormously with his honesty and genuine passion in classes.'"

Regardless of your age, how can you craft a life that allows you to engage your passions? Who will thank you later?

50s 'Wanna be Startin' Somethin'

Patrick Sheppard (1943-2019)

"When they were in their fifties, Patrick introduced Linda to the joys of overnight canoe trips, and for many years, they looked forward to planning their next summer excursions, just the two of them, often in Algonquin Park."

Algonquin Park in Ontario has 2,000 km of paddling and portage routes with 1,900 campsites along the way. Back then, Patrick and Linda would have slept in a tent, lugged around a Coleman stove and navigated with a compass (things have changed a lot in 20 years!). If we are willing to be a little uncomfortable our options for adventure are still wide open, even as our appreciation for a soft bed and pillow grows stronger.

Our families' camping mats have gotten a little thicker with each passing year. My latest, an Exped DownMat, has a layer of down nestled into its lining. Pop-up campers are starting to look pretty good. But the times I've been uncomfortable have turned out to be some of the most memorable of my life. I vow to remember this the next time I emerge from our tent to torrential rain with a screaming lower back.

> *What uncomfortable but memorable experiences have you had? Would you be willing to give up five stars for an entire sky full, even if it were only for one night?*

60s 'Stop In the Name of Love'

Jane S. Wood (1929-2019)

"She lived the phrase "It's better to be kind than to be right"
and she did so with great laughter, grace, wine and — until
she was 60 — cigarettes (which she gave up as her 60th
birthday present to her children)."

Jane's children clearly appreciate that their mom quit smoking. More importantly, that she quit smoking for them. I see this gift as many-fold: confirmation that Jane valued her own life, a show of how much she valued her kids, and an example of what one can do when they set their mind to it. It almost seems as if it was better to have smoked and quit than to have never smoked at all.

I am still working on giving up garage sales and thrift stores for my family. I love a good bargain and although sometimes they land on the winning side of my habit, they mostly can't stand the volume of my acquisitions. For me it's about more than "stuff." It's the random unexpected conversations I have with the people

I meet, the feel of old wood with wear spots from the hands of others or the tinge of mold I smell on a poetry book from yesteryear. If I follow Jane's lead I have more than a decade to indulge before I have to throw in the towel. I know I should probably concede and not put off until tomorrow what I can do today. But this is a hill I'm willing to die on. Besides, these kids are expensive and a little bit of hoarding seems like a small price to pay for being resourceful.

What bad habit can you kick in the name of those you love? For yourself?

70s 'These Boots' are made for walkin'

James Henry Forster (1918-2019)

"His love of hiking saw him climb Mount Kilimanjaro at age 79, travel to Base Camp Mount Everest and complete the Bruce Trail end to end (700 km) twice from the ages of 80-92 years."

According to the Mayo Clinic, the average American walks three to four thousand steps a day, or roughly one-and-a-half to two miles. At that rate completing the Bruce Trail would take a year and two months. We know that James was motivated far beyond average.

I'm not wired to want to conquer greatness of this magnitude, but I could pick a local trail and celebrate my half-century-old legs. I asked for a Fitbit as a birthday gift this year because of James. I was curious to see how many steps I walk in a single day. On a day that includes two dog walks I can hit my goal of eight thousand steps. If I keep increasing my daily goal it's feasible I could work my way to where James was at 79.

> *Do you have any ambitious, Kilimanjaro-sized goals to hit? What passion would press you to new heights?*

80s 'O Canada'

Timothy Hugh Hollick-Kenyon (1928-2019)

"He was recovering from strokes that diminished his mobility but left him fully his usual self: intelligent, irascible, fun-loving, extroverted and unendingly curious… Just last year, Tim voyaged to the Antarctic to add to his bird-sighting list and visit the area where his father flew and navigated for explorer Lincoln Ellsworth."

Tim was 88 when he made this sentimental pilgrimage, proof that he was thirsty for knowledge and experience until the very end. A shared sense of place can connect us to other people. Maybe this is why university and professional sport teams are so popular. In rooting for them we stand together with a sense of belonging and scream until our throats are sore, sometimes with paint on our faces maniacally waving bristol-board signs. Tim retracing the steps of his father into remote territory during his last year of life is a testimonial to how much we value place, people and our shared history.

I have honoured my own roots in the past several years by delving deeper into my family's Metis history. The stories of my Metis grandmothers took a backseat to those of their European husbands who had streets named after them for their contributions to early Winnipeg. These women with whom I share DNA were incredibly strong, wise and capable. Connecting myself to them has made me stronger. And very, very proud.

Are there stories from your family's history that you can draw fortitude from and then get thirsty for adventure?

90s   'The Times They are a-Changin'

Zora (Zoe) Elka Gropper (1918-2019)

> *"After [her husband] Natie died in 1996, Zoe's focus was on her growing family. She established a relationship with each of her 9 grandchildren and 14 great grandchildren. With the help of FaceTime, Facebook, Instagram and email, using her iPad, she kept in constant touch with them and shared their lives."*

Born in 1918, Zoe adapted from handwritten letters, to rotary phone, to live streaming, all in the name of connecting to those she loved. Zoe lived to be 101. She was proactive about being part of the lives of her grandchildren and great-grandchildren. When Facebook made its debut in 2004, Zoe was 86. When Instagram came onto the scene in 2010, Zoe was 92. By learning new technology she stayed relevant and reaped the rewards.

After reading Zoe's obituary I signed up for Snapchat and TikTok (social media apps). My husband and I posted a 20-second video on TikTok to test our social media legs. We wore funny hats, sang loudly and my husband even did some fancy footwork. Our 13- and 15-year-old sons diplomatically broke it to us: We had overstepped our boundaries in their burgeoning high school world. "Do what you want, just please don't use our family name." They drew their line in the sand. I am going to do my best to keep up with how my kids (and, maybe one day, grandkids) communicate. But I think I'll follow their lead rather than cut fresh tracks.

How can you stay relevant to continue to learn and expand your world, or to stay connected to the people you love?

100s 'Stayin' Alive'

Herbert Mosses Duguay (1914-2015)

"In the last few years, he was the goalie for the award-winning Bastion Care Home floor hockey team. Until two weeks ago, he walked up two flights of stairs each day."

Floor hockey at 100? That is a whole other level of *joie de vivre*. Because I was in disbelief, I did some digging to see if floor hockey at 100 is really a thing. It most certainly is; I even found a photo of a game between the Bastion Blazers and Hillside Silverheads in the *Salmon Arm Observer*. Players use classic plastic sticks to manoeuvre a soft puck between strategically positioned team members sitting on chairs. What really packs a punch in the photo is the intense faces on the men and women wielding hockey sticks. I can almost hear Herb goading on his opponents in jest and giving them a friendly slap on the back at the end of the game.

I spend a fair bit of time on the sidelines watching our kids play sports. Reading about Herb has me thinking about ways to work in some movement during this time that adds up to hours each week. As spectators we could resurrect The Wave from the 1980s and throw in celebratory jumping jacks, a few push-ups in camaraderie with the players and maybe even do the conga in the stands. The added bonus? Embarrassing our kids to help them build resilience.

What can you do to get back into the game? Are you going to "Let it Be" or are you ready to "Walk on the Wild Side?"

A page from Terry's book

Most people can identify a source of hardship from their lifetime, but few of us can relate to what Terry Fox and his family went through leading up to his death in 1981. Forty years later, Canadians are still running his *Marathon of Hope* every September and revering Terry for turning personal tragedy into a national movement in the fight against cancer.

I recently learned that Terry was inspired when he read an article about another amputee who ran in the New York City Marathon. His former basketball coach brought him the magazine article the night before his amputation. In Terry's words; "*It was then I decided to meet this new challenge head on and not only overcome my disability, but conquer it in such a way that I could never look back and say it disabled me*." Terry ran 5,373 kilometres through

Canada's Atlantic provinces, Quebec and Ontario before cancer in his lungs stopped him from running. Three million of us from around the globe continue to run for Terry each year.

The following obituaries profile the lives of people who faced hardships most of us can't imagine. But, much like Terry's story, they are filled with lessons on how to move forward when a challenge seems insurmountable. I think it's safe to say that none of these people were defined by their challenge. However, they were highly regarded for the way they lived their life despite the obstacles. Maybe you will find inspiration from the resilience of another person as Terry did more than four decades ago.

I am honoured to introduce you to each of these ten people with a valuable lesson to share.

Defy the odds as proof for others

Dorothy June Cherry (1926–2015)

"When Greg was born, he was diagnosed as having Muscular Dystrophy. The doctors told Mom not to love him because he would be crippled and probably die before he reached nine. He also suffered from colitis and croup and spent most of the first three years of his life in oxygen tents. Mom would hold him and rock him by the hour and doggedly determined, she taught him to walk. It took her the better part of three years, but he walked. Never underestimate the power of a mother's love."

June lived past her 89th birthday and was survived by Greg, so we can safely assume he lived beyond the age of nine!

What fed June's certainty that Greg could defy all expectations? Her own ability to defy what others deemed impossible must have played a role. Her own story is proof that odds can be beat and statistics can be scorned. June provided for her family as a single mother with a Grade 5 education. In her early years she "*worked as a hairdresser, later as an elevator operator, and then found her way into the payroll department at Woodward's. By age 23 she was Assistant Manager for a payroll of 5,000 employees.*" June was also a savvy Vancouver business woman, buying homes and dividing them into rental suites to fund her own mortgage, taxes and utilities.

If we know first-hand that we can defy the odds, we are in a strong position to believe that others can do the same. Not only was June a deeply committed and loving mother, she paved the way for possibility with her own exceptional feats.

> *What stories of defying the odds can you share to help empower others? Can you call upon the times you surprised yourself to fuel someone else's "impossible dream?"*

Refuse to be a victim

Lynn Ann Stewart (1955-2019)

"While in high school, Lynn narrowly survived a car accident in Boston and was told, as a paraplegic, she should limit her prospects. But Lynn dismissed this notion and found encouragement in many places; she vividly remembered hockey stars Bobby Orr and Derek Sanderson of the Bruins, calling her at the hospital in Boston and encouraging her to stay in school. No limits were accepted then or any time since."

Lynn was a member of the Canadian para-Olympic team in 1976 and won a bronze medal in table tennis. At sixteen, she started travelling and never stopped, attending five universities from coast to coast in Canada and one in Belgium on a scholarship. With a Ph.D. in Clinical Psychology from York University she began a lifelong career in forensic psychology working for Corrections Canada. Her expertise led to many engagements at national and international forums as an ambassador for the Canadian correctional system.

Navigating a new university campus far from home is a harrowing experience for most young people. Can you imagine doing it six times at six different campuses, each time in a wheelchair? Wheelchair ramps, automatic doors and accessible washrooms were few and far between when Lynn was in university. Reading Lynn's obituary leaves little room for excuses not to participate. Not now, not ever.

When has someone said "you can't do that"? What did you do to prove them wrong?

Expand your definition of mentor

Bruce Colin Binnie (1941-2019)

"By the early 90s, Bruce was very fortunate to be able to move to Beth Tikvah, a new group home in Westdale for developmentally disabled older adults. This became a secure and much loved home for him. Bruce was definitely a part of his community, involved in a myriad of activities, riding his bike, having coffee, meeting everyone in Westdale. He was always the friendliest person in the room and introduced himself to all he met."

Bruce's great-niece, Laura Vander Steen, writes about trips to stay with Bruce and her great-grandmother on his tribute page:

"Bruce and I baked (on his strong encouragement), spent time counting his pennies, picking mint for gram's boiled new potatoes and watched as the jell-o set on the porch

in the cold late winter days. He would sit in his deep olive green La-Z-Boy and watch wrestling and always share his chips and I poured his strong tea from a miniature tea set. Bruce always encouraged my "experiments" and would exclaim me a "genius" for my tin foil creations that mostly resembled alien monuments. Bruce would plea for Gram to take us downtown for a shamrock shake, a request she always honoured. Bruce shared his cocoa puffs and made me feel like I had a true grown-up friend."

Bruce's life lessons are dedicated to anyone who thinks the only way to be a mentor is to achieve a certain level of education or a professional title. Laura took us with her back to her childhood so that we could meet Bruce. We are better for knowing him through her eyes.

Have you had a mentor that breaks the stereotype of older and more educated? Is there a friendliest person in a place you frequent that you could learn from?

Focus on the good stuff

John Davidson Brown, M.D., Ph.D., FRCP(C) (1938-2009)

"He worked most nights and every weekend but graduated from medicine with no debt, one shirt and one pen."

John's life started hard. By age ten he had spent years in the hospital for polio and other health problems. His mother, who nursed him through these stays, died shortly after he returned home. By the age of 15 he was self-sufficient. He put himself through university and medical school (Manitoba), working as a baker, a bartender, and a laboratory assistant. He won the Prowse Prize for his Ph.D. (Manitoba) and studied at the National Hospital for Neurological Diseases (London) as a Medical Research Council Fellow. When his wife of 45 years could no longer fight the cancers that had plagued her for more than a decade, he cared for her at home. *"Although exhausted* *and heartbroken he would never describe this time as anything but a privilege."*

John must have picked himself up in the midst of his grief to start putting one foot in front of the other with unimaginable resolve. Did he carry a photo of his mother and steal moments alone to bask in her memory and imagine the life she wanted for him? Instead of feeling self-pity for the time spent in hospital as a boy did John use gratitude as the impetus to become a neurologist? When he cared for his wife in her final years did he draw upon the nurturing he received at the hands of his mother and caregivers? Did he lay a warm washcloth on her forehead and brush her hair? It seems John stayed tender despite a series of life experiences that would have hardened most people. The biggest lesson I take from John is that being heartbroken is a privilege. Our heart can't break if it's tucked away in a safe place.

What good thing(s) about you or someone you know took root during a time of hardship? How can you stay tender when you want to put on your armour?

Recreate yourself

William Hawkins (1940-2016)

*"In the 70s Bill's star dimmed for a time but was never
extinguished. After dealing with addiction issues, he
reinvented himself as the capital's most literate cab
driver, with regular clients among politicians, judges and
journalists."*

His obituary opens with the line "*Canada has lost an artist that
inspired two generations of writers and musicians.*" According
to CBC News, "From 1964 to 1971 Hawkins published five
collections of poetry and also had an impact on the Ottawa
music scene where he performed in bands alongside musicians
such as Bruce Cockburn and Darius Brubeck."

I can imagine Bill behind the steering wheel pointing out where
the famous Cafe Le Hibou once stood in Ottawa around the
corner from the Parliament buildings. Maybe he rubbed elbows
with George Harrison when the famous Beatle stopped by in

1969. I imagine him reciting one of his poems using his rear view mirror to make eye contact with his customers in the back seat. Maybe he regaled them with stories of Leonard Cohen, or the day Jimi Hendrix stopped in to watch Joni Mitchell perform there.

Bill was a true Ambassador for our Nation's Capital on behalf of cab drivers everywhere. He didn't let his detour with addiction stop him from taking the road less travelled.

What unexpected route can you take that leads to a more enriching life? Have you already taken an unexpected route that enriched your life?

Educate others about ability

Barbara Ann Winfield (1942-2019)

"For many years, Barb and her friends with disabilities illustrated their unique talents at elementary school assemblies in order to teach children the true meaning of accessibility and resiliency. Barb's passionate interest in mouth painting and resultant demonstrated skills were a testament to just what possibility and fortitude could accomplish. Using her voice-activated computer, Barb not only managed her own personal affairs but also recruited volunteers each year to staff and support a variety of community events such as the Port Hope Jazz Festival, the town library elevator fundraiser, and the annual participation in, and fundraising of, her 'Motley Majestics' team to benefit the MS Walk. All of her endeavours exemplified Barb's incredible skill and patience in "rallying the troops" to help make Port Hope the great community it is today."

Barb was diagnosed with multiple sclerosis in her early 40s. Despite her weakening condition over the years and her need for a motorized wheelchair for daily living, she volunteered for a multitude of local causes and was recognized for her significant involvement and contribution.

Barb could have opted to be idle. But she didn't. I like to imagine Barb turning up the volume on her voice-activated computer to recruit volunteers from among the bustling downtown lunch-hour crowd on a sunny day. I see curious elementary school students with paint brushes clenched between their teeth, sampling the taste of artistic freedom. I hear thunderous clapping while people rise to their feet at the conclusion of a mouth painting demonstration to express their awe of Barb and her ability. Barb inspired people with disabilities, dispelled myths about the limitations of a disability and modelled resilience for young people of all abilities.

What personal challenge can you reframe to enable others to see possibility in adversity?

Find beauty in the midst of chaos

Margaret Jordis Nokleberg (1928-2019)

"Hallucinations and paranoia (early undiagnosed dementia) crept into her life like a bad neighbour. A cloud of chaos and dread unsettled the family, and we became a Nordic soap opera. But for all the trauma and tragedy, she loved life and prized its little and precious moments. A good cup of coffee at a fine restaurant. A sentimental musical. Boating on Drag Lake. Sitting by the beach in Costa Rica. Laughing about ridiculous things. The unconditional love of dogs. Anything about Norway. In many ways she prized the best of Norwegian virtues: courage, honesty, hard work, fidelity, hospitality, self-reliance and perseverance."

Margaret continued to love life and prize moments in the midst of chaos, and this did not go unnoticed by those who loved her. I especially appreciate the acknowledgment of the "Norwegian virtues" that Margaret embodied because it sees Margaret the way she would choose to be seen, using the measuring stick of the culture she identified with. Likening her hallucinations and paranoia to a "bad neighbour" reminds us that Margaret and her illness were separate from one another. Margaret was not her illness and her children have made this clear.

What joy can you find in the midst of chaos? How do you find it?

Reject the diagnosis

Diana Hamer-Jackson (1936-2019)

"Mom was diagnosed with ovarian cancer six months after Calvin was born and although she was told she would most likely succumb to the disease she replied 'I can't leave, I have six babies to take care of', and that she did."

Diana bucked the odds in a big way, living until she was 83. Ovarian cancer is the most lethal women's cancer. Today about 55 percent of people with ovarian cancer die within five years of diagnosis. Diana's odds of survival were much lower in the 1960s. Some people would attribute her long life to a mind-body connection while others call it "luck." Regardless, she taught us that words like "odds" and "probabilities" are another way of saying "we don't know for sure." Imagine if she had stopped nestling her nose in the flock of hair on her newborn's head or gave up reading to her toddlers at bedtime because she was fixated on her impending end. She didn't, and this has become a life lesson for all of us.

> *Have you ever rejected a diagnosis? Do you chalk up beating the odds to luck or something more?*

Grow deep

Zachary Schylore Laird (1997–2010)

"After a long and courageous battle with brain cancer, Zach passed away peacefully in the early morning of May 2nd. His light shone out to the world until his very last breath... As his body wasted away, his spirit grew stronger and more beautiful."

I like to imagine that Zach grew to be aware of the spirit that glowed from the deepest depths of his being. That he felt the light he exuded to others return to him many-fold. That in his 13 years he might have learned what many of us never learn in a lifetime; That a short, deep life is more abundant than a long, shallow one.

What if we consider life in the context of volume (volume = length x width x depth) rather than measuring it as a linear timeline? If we shorten its length we can still achieve the same volume. How? We increase our depth. We go deeper into our thought, purpose and connection to others. In the context of volume, Zach lived a life of epic proportions.

I wish for Zach, and his family, that he had lived a longer life. But Zach didn't need a long life to gift us inspiration for living more deeply and purposefully with whatever life we have left.

Is there a shift that you can make to increase your inner depth?

Disappointment is part of the process

R.A. Gordon McGee (1954–2019)

"At age 23 he started life over in a wheelchair. Gord and Becca married in 1978 [the following year] and Gord Jr. was born soon thereafter. In the ensuing 41 years Gord faced every challenge with his legendary physical strength and indomitable spirit. There were remarkable successes; through sheer force of will he swam, boated, explored, travelled and drove everywhere, attracting an army of admiring friends, helpers and supporters from all walks of life. But there were also many frustrations and disappointments born of his disability including his attempts to relaunch his career in commercial real estate and to become a teacher after earning his certificate in education at UBC. After a period of mounting self-doubt and self-recrimination, Gord found peace and inspiration in his Christian faith, which helped to strengthen and guide him for the rest of his life."

Driving to Edmonton from Vancouver for an exciting new position in real estate development, Gord hit black ice. He broke his back in the car accident and became paralyzed.

Gord was staring paraplegia straight in the face two decades before Christopher Reeve made the terms quadriplegic, paraplegic and spinal cord injury commonplace. Today there are approximately 86,000 Canadians living with a spinal cord injury. Each year brings 4,300 new cases, and men represent eighty percent of these cases.

Today a quick Google of "living with a spinal cord injury" yields pages of results. Glossy magazine articles, chat rooms for parents and reviews of the latest wheelchair-friendly products can be found with the click of a touch pad. As a newlywed man with a newborn in the late 70s, however, there would have been little information to help Gord navigate the new realities of his life with paraplegia. And no information about parenting with paraplegia.

The important role of faith in Gord's life after the accident is mentioned more than once in his obituary. It is impossible to fathom the emotions Gord must have felt navigating paraplegia, marriage and a new baby in the span of just six months. Devastation. Elation. Hopelessness. Joy. Uncertainty. He turned to a higher power and in turn, his faith provided Gord with indomitable strength.

I appreciate acknowledgement of the intense determination that enabled Gord to do and experience so much despite the hurdles. But I appreciate even more the honesty about how frustrating and difficult those hurdles were.

> *Can you be honest about your frustrations to let others know they are not alone?*

Late bloomers

Life unfolds in stages and with each stage comes different responsibilities. Sure, you can push the boundaries and run that Ironman when your kids are young or take up skydiving during your bar exams. But if you're not a maximizer, why not allow yourself to bask in the things that come with your stage of life and also accept the limitations that come with it? Take a lesson from flowers. Asters keep a low profile all summer long and take centre stage with spectacular blooms in the autumn.

The old adage "live like there is no tomorrow" doesn't acknowledge that today you still need to stock your fridge with milk, deal with a colicky baby, get your tires changed or pop into the office to finish up some paperwork.

If we knew we had tomorrow would we find greater contentment in the mediocrity of today? How can we find contentment in the mundane aspects of life? Regardless of our response to these questions, we all grapple with the possibility of limited time. How do we strike a balance between living larger-than-life and embracing the simple things? I try to immerse myself in the responsibilities I face each day with the hope that I can tackle my bucket list later. If later doesn't come, I will know I didn't fetter my days away trying to be somewhere else doing something else when I could have lived the present moment more fully. Can a string of ordinary days ever add up to an extraordinary life?

A headline in my *CBC News Brief* caught my eye last week; "Vancouver man will be the oldest qualified runner at the 2020 Boston Marathon." Rod Waterlow, an 82-year-old Vancouverite, didn't start running until he was 47. It was an idea that came to him over a St. Patrick's Day beer with a friend who was training for the Vancouver Marathon. My intrigue is less about Rod qualifying for the Boston Marathon at 82, and more about his foray into running at 47. Why? Because this story shouts out "it's not too late for you Tamara!" It's a kick in the aster to remain open to the possibility of being exceptional at something.

These ten people were fortunate that a long, able life allowed them to tackle some of their most memorable experiences in their later years. Each of them offer us a lesson.

Build it and they will come

Burnice Lucille (Lou) Davis (1930-2017)

"After the sudden passing of her husband Russell, Lou went on to build and operate the Lost Erra Resort and Trailer Park in Campbell River, BC from 1970-1981... Lou was an influential icon in the post-war modern women's rights movement and became the first woman in North America to hold a licensed Blaster's Certificate."

In 1958 Lou and her husband were engineers in the planning of the world's largest non-atomic blast in Ripple Rock, Campbell River, B.C. Together they owned C.I.L. Explosives and Accessories where Lou handled all types of explosives.

Losing her husband prompted Lou to explore new possibilities. I can imagine Lou's walk on the property at Campbell River trying to imagine life there as a widow while her business vision took shape in her mind. Later she might have driven around the grounds on a four-wheeler and hauled her tool box out of the back to bang up some 2x4s to frame a public washroom. I imagine her enthusiastically welcoming back regular customers by day, and strolling around with a flashlight to enforce the "no noise after 10 p.m." policy with a firm voice by night.

I recently came home with my first houseplant. My husband looked at it and said "I don't think we can handle any more dependents right now." I laughed, but I understood completely. Over the past 15 years we have been building our nest and filling it with kids, their friends, wayward second-hand pets and a miscellany of young adults in transition for chunks of time. We are only recently enjoying the freedom that comes with kids who ditch us for an evening with their friends. We are starting to see the possibilities of a future that doesn't tie us to a particular lifestyle or home. Lou is a wonderful example of how to live and earn a living on your own terms.

> *What long-held business vision would you bring to fruition if you had the resources or if your life circumstances changed?*

Career shifting isn't just for millennials

Noel Michael Bernard (1957-2019)

"He also had a variety of job occupations in his lifetime; Noel worked for Parks Canada in Cheticamp, was a former RCMP officer for Baddeck RCMP Detachment, a lobster fisherman, a proud owner of the previous Kwikway Store and served his community as a Wagmatcook Band Councillor for a number of years."

Noel was known to be an inspiration for youth and a role model to many. I like to imagine him sharing entertaining stories with young people about his various jobs. Maybe he told them about a close encounter with a bear. I imagine him explaining how he identified male lobsters by their crusher claw intended to attract a mate. I see him sharing tips on how to show others that you are listening to them and representing their voice at the decision-making table. Most of us spend much of the waking hours of our adult life working. Noel shows us that work can be part of what makes life an adventure rather than waiting for the adventure to begin after we punch out at the end of the day.

What if we thought of life as a smörgåsbord and sampled as much as possible, but also allowed ourselves to save room for the things we enjoy the most? It seems Noel did just this and also considered how he could be of greatest service to others in the five careers spanning his 61 years of life.

What career or job can you take a bite of, even if it's just a small taste? What subject are you curious about that could lead to a new line of work?

Drummer, Dancer, Artist: Take your pick

Patricia Marilyn MacKay (1924-2019)

"Her sights were firmly set on the future. She was always excited to learn new things, and pursue new hobbies; birdwatching, ballroom dancing, pottery, weaving, drumming — her enthusiasm never waned."

Pat was a strong matriarch who put family above all else. She also gave her time generously to more than a dozen national and community organizations, often being elected to the role of chair in recognition of her compassion and practicality. She was an ardent supporter of organizations that advocated for youth, vulnerable families and people at risk. She dedicated decades of her life to building inclusive communities where every person was valued and provided for without exception. She was awarded the Order of Canada in 1984 for these contributions.

Later in life, she found time to explore new hobbies and interests. I see her throwing clay and spinning a mug to serve hot chocolate in when grandkids came to visit. I imagine her banging on the drums and enjoying the solidarity that comes with a group of people working together in unison, a value she embodied her entire life.

There is an added bonus when we continue to explore and learn beyond meeting new people and having fun. A recent Harvard Medical School study shows that new brain cell growth can happen in late adulthood with the process of learning and acquiring new information and experiences.

How can you go with the flow and be open to interests, skills and hobbies that find you later in life?

Start an inclusive club

John Robert (Bob) Chittick (1926-2019)

"His retired Toronto years also included membership in the ROMEOs (Retired Old Men Eating Out) lunch club and then, the Cane Club which required members to be at least 80 years old and own a cane ... although none of Bob's family can ever recall him owning one."

Even during his prime work years, Bob *"always prioritized family and friends."* As co-founder of Web Offset Publications, carving out time beyond the work day would have been no small task. This was the company chosen to print the Western and Eastern Canada copies of the *The Globe and Mail* when it became Canada's first national newspaper in 1981. Bob *"could be counted on to back up warm words with effort, ideas and solutions to make things better."* These are attributes that anyone would be fortunate to have in a friend at any stage of life. Creating a new reason to get together as life evolved (ie. a non-existent cane), ensured that Bob and his buddies were able to enjoy camaraderie and their collective wisdom long after being social was structured around work days and tee off time.

My husband recently returned home from a day ripping with friends on his dirt bike unable to bear weight on his leg. It was the third strike, and the third trip to the pharmacy to rent a rolling knee scooter. He immediately listed his bike for sale, and over the next fews days his dirt bike buddies popped by as disappointment hung in the air. I soon realized that it wasn't the loss of dirt-biking that my husband lamented. It was the camaraderie of these men that he feared losing. A constructive optimist, my husband stated that he'd find a new way to gather up "the dirt bags" to enjoy their philosophical meanderings and shared time in the mystery "nothing box."

> *How can you pull together the people you enjoy in a way that doesn't require climbing mountains (or moving them)?*

Party like it's 1999 – even if you are 99

Dr. Dagmar Vosu (1917-2019)

"She was an avid traveller, and for many years celebrated New Years in the Canary Islands with friends from Sweden. Dagmar enjoyed the opera and theatre, and was a regular at the Shaw and Stratford festivals."

Dagmar valued friendship and nurtured it. She stayed active in her sorority throughout her life. Upon retirement she moved to a co-op where she *"loved to arrange large parties as much as she loved to attend them."*

I have been part of a book club for 18 years. At our first gathering we all fawned over the first newborn of the bunch who breastfed during our discussion. Since that day we have celebrated the arrival of 23 babies, the youngest now 13. We have supported each other through losses and gains too many to count. I value friendship deeply, just as Dagmar did, and book club makes friendship easy. This group of women forms a supportive, interesting and interested posse, shows up once each month at a pre-designated time and doesn't require regular contact as proof they are valued. We take turns hosting and the only requirement is that the host serves something sweet and has toilet paper. It has made sustained and intimate friendship possible in my world of contract work, shift work, school-age kids and no extended family support nearby. I hope to grow old(er) with this wonderful group of humans. Maybe years from now we will stay up late watching movies, eating popcorn with extra butter and have sleepovers on the pull-out couch. Something tells me Dagmar and her friends did.

> *What do you value most in friendships? How can you strengthen the bonds you have to weather the years?*

Unleash your moxie

Theresa Joyce (1935-2019)

*"She earned her pilot license and became a member of
the Ninety-Nines women's flying organization in her early
forties. She moved to Japan for a year to teach English in
her late fifties, got her motorcycle license when she was 72,
moved to the country of Panama at 74 before settling back
to Ontario at the age of 79."*

Theresa had moxie. She spent time in an orphanage as a child
and her *"wild spirit bloomed early"* when she married at the age
of 17. Later, as a single mom of two, she made ends meet working
as a secretary. When she married Ron Joyce in her mid-twenties,
their entrepreneurial spirits were fuelled by the need to support
their blended family—soon to include three more children. They
purchased a Dairy Queen franchise with money Theresa had
saved and the help of a loan. With a baby in her arms, and soon a
baby and toddler, Theresa worked the store full-time. Later this

same dogged work ethic helped grow the Canadian icon that Tim Hortons is today.

When I read Theresa's obituary I wonder how she had enough stamina left in the tank to take big bites out of life after 40 (and a second divorce). Perhaps the answer lies in the likening of her life to *"that of a rollercoaster."* A rollercoaster relies on steep drops to gather the kinetic energy required to hurtle uphill. Enough energy is generated by the up and down motion of a rollercoaster to keep it in perpetual motion. Perhaps Theresa's milestone feats of her 40's, 50s, 60's and 70's were fuelled by the rollercoaster of life, teeming with peaks and valleys.

With a 13- and 15-year-old at home I'm still in the throws of routine, but Theresa promises that my fireball years will come. Knowing this helps me to be in the moment with my growing family as the years start to slip through my fingers at Mach speed. Theresa has also illuminated the need to put some moxie in reserve for when I surface.

> *Have your fireball years arrived? If not, take a minute to imagine what they might look like. How will you access the moxie needed to continue to take big bites out of life?*

Be a world citizen without leaving home

Johanna Helfinger (1930-2019)

*"One of her most memorable enthusiasms was for Ireland —
its history, people, and music. During this phase she sought
out Irish people, making friends and charming (as well as
frightening) them with her zeal."*

Johanna proves it will never be too late to quench your curiosity
about other cultures and places. If we all run out of carbon credits
and airplane travel becomes obsolete, we can take a page from
Johanna's life and discover that it's possible to explore another
culture without leaving the country.

We are enjoying the new family on our street. They recently
explained the meaning behind Diwali, the Hindu festival of
lights, while their kids circled around us, one on a bike, one
chasing the one on a bike. This fall we marvelled at the front
window of their home as it played host to dozens of candles that
lit up the joyous faces of their friends and family gathering to

celebrate. Our street had never accommodated so many parked cars and neighbours in every direction were curious about what had brought so many people on a weekday evening in November. I loved learning about this beautiful ceremony and last week we received an invitation for a home-cooked Indian meal. The spiritual symbolic celebration on our cul-de-sac brought with it all that Diwali symbolizes: "victory of light over darkness, good over evil, and knowledge over ignorance."

What place, culture or festivals can you explore without using carbon credits? Do you have neighbours or work colleagues who might be a starting point?

You can even stop late

Della Jean Wagner Conquergood (1917–2019)

"She began her career at the Eaton Co., retiring from Henry Birks at age 80."

I can imagine Della helping a nervous young man choose an engagement ring, her years of experience guiding her to point out the ones within his budget. I hear her soft, self-assured voice offering advice on how to ask for the woman's hand in marriage from the father. Maybe she explained how to gently cup the palm of the soon-to-be fiancé to nudge the ring on while looking her in the eyes. Della lived to be 102. It seems safe to assume that her job played a role in keeping her mind and body strong.

There is no magic button that turns off our career motor at 65 years old. Della reminds us that we are only limited by convention. Heck, using her formula, you could start your career at 65 and still work a solid 15 years. That's the same number of years I worked before I took a break to grow a family, and to me those years felt like a lifetime. Sure I put in many long days, but I grew a wide skill set, made many lifelong friends and had a strong sense of belong at each of several work places spanning two provinces and one territory.

What do you enjoy enough to keep doing long after people expect you to stop?

Be Romeo to your Juliet – Or vice versa

Rudolf Helfinger (1926-2014)

*"The stress of looking after Johanna eventually killed him.
Throughout his final days in hospital, he thought only about
her."*

Rudolf cared for his wife Johanna and *"loved her with every inch
of his soul"* when Alzheimers began to *"blot out her personality."*
Now that you have met Johanna (in the pages of this book) you
can understand how easy it must have been to love her. Rudolf
gave everything for the woman he loved including his life. He
died a month after falling ill in the midst of tending to her every
need. Johanna died five years later, reuniting this Juliet with her
Romeo.

When we speak of Romeo and Juliet we refer to the ultimate story
of love; two young lovers who choose death over a life without
one another. But studies show it's older lovers who are most
deeply affected by the death of their partner. The "widowhood

effect" refers to the increased likelihood of a spouse dying in the months following the death of their husband or wife. A 2013 study revealed a 66 percent increased chance of dying during the first three months after a spouse's death. Grief is an obvious contributor, but physicians also point to the surviving spouse paying less attention to their own health and well-being as their partners' health deteriorates. Rudolf, who was known as *"a consummate gentleman and man of integrity,"* put caring for Johanna ahead of his own well-being. He was a true Romeo at the age of 88.

What lengths would you go to for your Romeo or Juliet?
What lengths have you already gone?

Throw a curve ball

Annette Elizabeth Wanless (1928-2019)

"... she even tried her hand at Dragon boating, but not until reaching the tender age of 71."

Annette was firmly rooted in her role of mom, nurse and was *"an avid gardener, writer of letters, needle-pointer, knitter and reader,"* so her go at being part of a team that propels a 40-foot boat forward stands out in her obituary.

Annette remained resiliant through her battle with breast cancer and stayed "positive to the very end of her descent into Alzheimer's." I am comforted to learn that a tender and creative soul like Annette was able to stand strong in battle when life required it of her. I like to imagine her gently putting down her knitting needles and pulling on a pair of boxing gloves with a "just try me" glint in her eye. As a kindred creative spirit I hope that I would be able to do the same.

Have you discovered a super power during a crisis in your life? What strengths lie below your surface that you could call into action during a time of need?

Pay it forward for our Veterans

NOVEMBER

November is earmarked to honour veterans and peacekeepers who have made unfathomable sacrifices (44,090 Canadian soldiers gave their life in the Second World War alone) so that we can live in freedom. They have endured cold trenches, gut-piercing hunger and overwhelming uncertainty on behalf of millions of people. Here's an idea: As an expression of our gratitude for their sacrifice, consider dedicating two minutes a day to make the life of another person a little better, whether you know them or not.

In *Born to Be Good*, Dacher Keltner suggests that "survival is not a matter of who is the fittest, but who is the kindest." His work speaks to the importance of "the simplest of touches and the slightest of smiles" to engage with others and to form cooperative communities.

A study done at The University of British Columbia asked children aged nine to eleven to perform various acts of kindness over the course of four weeks. They found that not only did the children doing these acts get happier over time, but they also became more popular with their peers. A positive spin-off was more inclusive behaviours and less externalizing behaviours (i.e. less bullying) for youth that participated.

When we purposefully direct our attention to another human, even briefly, we tell them they matter. The following obituaries shed light on ways we can show others they are seen and valued. When a gesture is noted in an obituary we know it had an impact on the lives of others. Most of these small but poignant offerings don't even require an exchange of words.

Maybe the best way to honour our veterans is to work to create a world where war is unnecessary. Perhaps if more of us sacrificed more in little ways, fewer people would be called upon to sacrifice so much.

Each of these ten people found a way to pay it forward with small gestures that were appreciated by others. The investment of time? Two minutes or less.

Stop for lemonade

Herbert Mosses Duguay (1914-2015)

"Herb never walked past a child's lemonade stand without buying a glass and chatting."

Herb started a business in the 1950s that sold products to building supply stores across Western Canada. He was well-respected for his ethics and the relationships he nurtured as a travelling salesman. Herb must have found it impossible to resist stopping to support a budding young entrepreneur behind a table adorned with a hand-lettered "lemonade for sale" sign. I can imagine Herb asking "how is business today?" and offering words of encouragement. Did he offer advice on reinvesting the profits or did he indulge the young entrepreneur's hopes of a big splurge?

A lemonade stand is often a child's first crack at independence. They have to gather supplies, consider profit margins, promote their wares and get comfortable talking to people they've never met. By going to these lengths to test out their entrepreneurial legs they are signalling their readiness for interactions and transactions. It seems a wonderful time to stop and take notice of a young person. By doing so we become part of their journey towards independence.

Opportunities for kids to talk to seniors are diminishing as the geographical spread between families grows and retirement communities increasingly segregate seniors. Kids who sold Herb a lemonade ended up with far more than a pocketful of change. They experienced an interaction with a *"friendly, funny, honest and kind-hearted"* human who was widely known as a *"man of worth."*

> *How can you dedicate a few minutes to support a young person who is testing the waters of the bigger world?*

Wave

George Robert Demidoff (1934-2019)

"For his last few years, he enjoyed sitting in his smoking
porch and waving at the dog walkers as they went by. He
especially enjoyed his almost daily visits from neighbour
Pete and his dog Gus. There was always a biscuit for Gus!"

So much goodness delivered, and George didn't even need to
get out of his chair (except maybe to get the biscuits). I imagine
Gus tugging on his leash as they neared George's house. I like
to imagine his tail wagging uncontrollably as George unscrewed
the lid of the biscuits, whining softly if it took too long. I see
Gus sitting at attention and taking the treat gently from George's
open hand. I feel certain Gus, Pete and many other neighbours
continue to look in the direction of George's empty porch on
their neighbourhood walks.

I had my own version of George as a child. We drove Manitoba's
Highway 59 through the Brokenhead Ojibway Nation to

get to my grandparents' cabin on Lake Winnipeg. For years an older gentleman sat on a chair at the side of the highway in this community and waved to passersby. I would press my nose against the smudged window of our station wagon to anticipate "the waver" miles before reaching his usual spot. As we approached I would pour everything I had into my wave back to him, resembling more of a dance move than a wave. One day he made eye contact with me and that moment is etched in my memory. He. Saw. Me.

Note: I recently discovered a CBC article from 2018 that reveals there were actually two "wavers." These retired brothers would sit in lawn chairs and wave for as many as 10 hours each day.

Someone always has to be the first to wave. Will it be you?

Connect people to each other

George S.B. Moad (1946-2019)

"Armed with a Rolodex of business cards from everyone he ever met, he thought nothing of approaching people who might normally have never given him the time of day. He had a real knack of connecting people in need with the right people to help."

There is no app that will ever connect people the way someone with a *"kind and generous heart"* who befriends people from all walks of life can. George was an *"expert networker"* who constantly met decision-makers and change-makers in his role as an entrepreneur and community volunteer. He started a typing school for unemployed women, was a scout leader to hundreds of boys, helped rescue dogs, organized community events like the Santa Claus parade, and the list goes on. As an example of his panache for reaching out to *"people who might normally have never given him the time of day,"* he arranged for Anne Murray to be the Honorary Chief Parade Marshall for the 1970 Grey Cup. One can only imagine how many dots George connected and the shape they have taken — and will continue to take — over time. He was laid to rest wearing his *Patton* T-shirt with the theme from the movie *Patton* playing. In his review of *Patton*, film critic Roger Ebert writes "Patton is not a war film so much as the story of a personality who has found the right role to play." We never got to meet George but we know that he, too, found the right role to play.

We can take a page from George's book and look beyond age, gender and power status when we consider how to connect people to each other. One of my favourite things about living in Iqaluit, Nunavut in my 30s was the diversity. I learned some karate beside a five-year-old and his grandmother. I played hockey on a team with a gaggle of 13-year-old girls and a 62-year-old woman. I took a jewellery-making class taught by a male Inuk artist. Social media aims to connect like with like, but I find life to be richer when we mingle with others who bring a perspective that is etched by an entirely different set of life experiences.

> *Which people can you connect that might be able to help each other? Would you be willing to take a leap and follow up with a suggested contact provided by someone else?*

Welcome tag alongs

Michael L.G. Joy (1940-2020)

"He was a man of many interests who always had time for the numerous children who would follow him like shadows as he puttered on his latest amazing project."

**Mike *"imparted his love of nature,* *enquiry and adventure on his young assistants, whether tinkering on his jet boat Feeble, constructing a zip line, building model rockets, fishing or going on long walks where 'getting lost' was all part of the fun."* As a pioneer in the development of Magnetic Resonance and Electric Current Density Imaging. Mike must have appreciated the strength of hands-on learning. It's hard to fathom the depth of knowledge that rubbed off on his young assistants as they explored and created alongside this University of Toronto professor emeritus.

Few people are able to turn the *"most mundane chore into both an adventure and a learning experience."* Mike shared his passion for learning by giving others an opportunity to explore at their own pace. We don't need to imprint our own knowledge onto others to be a teacher.

When other people are enjoying something, we get curious. When I lived in Iqaluit, Nunavut I fell in love with how Inuk parents teach their children about life on the land. Few words are exchanged, instead children watch their parents attentively as they do what is required to build a quamotiq (wooden sled), stretch an animal hide or prepare pitsi (dried arctic char). Over time the children get more involved with their own hands until the parent can step back and watch. As a bystander I have felt the genuine enthusiasm that drives this process. There are no parental monologues or reminders to "pay attention!" because the kids are fuelled by their own curiosity and the enthusiasm of their parent.

What skills and knowledge can you share with others by inviting them to stand beside you as you toil and create?

Let others know you see them

J. Alexander Langford Q.C. (1931-2019)

"Every grandchild knew his distinctive wink."

Alex deeply valued academics and *"never travelled without a suitcase full of books."* He sat in the *"tallest seat at the family table"* and had a *"profound sense of occasion, the more pomp and circumstance the better!"* Would this cultured gent play a practical joke on someone when they excused themselves from the table — maybe turn their cutlery upside down — and use the wink to seal the secret with the grandchild sitting across the table? Was his wink so subtle and quick it eluded his wife and adult children? Did his grandchildren stand in front of the mirror and spend hours trying to mimic his wink?

Someone told me to "look each of your children in the eye at least once a day." When our kids were younger, and the days much longer, I often went to bed wracking my brain to recall if I had done this. A wink would seal the deal and confirm the transaction completed.

> *What small gesture can you use to show your loved ones they are a member in the exclusive club of people you adore?*

Honour with a name

Evelyn Mitchell (1933-2019)

*"Even in her last days she took care to let you know that the baby is Rosalie **Evelyn**. Let's be clear."*

It takes just seconds to add a middle name (or names) to a birth certificate application form, but the magnitude of honour bestowed is immeasurable. In Canada "name act" laws are a provincial matter. In Quebec, for example, "it is recommended to limit the number of given names to four."

But naming honours aren't limited to babies. We have a room in our home dedicated to a friend we met in Iqaluit, Nunavut who kept her home open to children from morning until night. She doled out an endless supply of healthy snacks. Her kitchen table was always equipped with paint and good-quality paper for anyone who took an interest (and there were many). Years ago I stood on a wobbly stool and painted "The Beth McKenty Room," on a wall spanning one side of the dedicated room to the other. The quality of the hand-painted letters is dicey, but they honour and remind us of an exceptional human.

> *If you're finished naming babies is there something else you could name in honour of someone you feel is pretty exceptional?*

Share your awe

George Ernest Gould (1924-2017)

"His sense of wonder — one of the many gifts he passed on to his children and grandchildren — was expressed through stargazing and a passion for cosmology."

Does George's love of the sky stem from growing up in a small Saskatchewan village in the 1920s where he walked Bessie the cow out to pasture each day and *"earned his first dimes running messages from the post office when a phone call came through for someone in town"*? Did he lie on his back in the long prairie grass and look at the starlit sky with his father and ask questions about the size of the universe? He may have sought out those familiar constellations when he flew light bombers with the RCAF in the Second World War. Did his heart ache when he was studying Actuarial Science at University of Manitoba where too many city lights masked the clarity of the stars? How long after he met his wife-to-be Joan Anne did he direct her gaze up beyond the tall buildings of Toronto to introduce her to his sky?

Knowledge can be finite but wonder is infinite. By gifting a *"sense of wonder"* to his children and grandchildren there is no limit to where it will take them. A sense of wonder makes us thirsty for understanding and so we seek answers to quench our thirst. To share wonder we have to make our curiosity about the things that give us awe infectious. George infused two generations with wonder.

| *How can you infuse future generations with your awe?*

Create space for others to flourish

Eileen Mary Hawryliw (1926-2018)

"Eileen's tireless exuberant nature complemented and contrasted with that of the quiet, steady demeanour of her beloved Bohan. She gave freedom and space to his own personality, and to those of her sons.... Her steadfast encouragement to sense new opportunities, to accomplish meaningful and rewarding goals applied to them and to herself."

Eileen and Bohan married in Saskatchewan in 1953 *"not only because of their similar ancestral roots in Western Ukraine, but because of their shared, unadvertised passion for an open road, an open mind and a house with an open door."* I appreciate the reminder that shared values lie at the root of many successful life partnerships. However, similar personalities are not required. The different but complementary personalities of Eileen and Bohan are front and centre in the description of their move from rural living to urban land-lording. Bohan managed maintenance and repairs and Eileen's *"fondness for conversation was irrepressible and she eagerly opened the Hawryliw home offering their myriad of tenants coffee, cookies and a good catch-up in exchange for next month's rent."* It's a good thing that her most prized keepsakes were the *"experiences she shared"* and not ones that required money.

After ten years of marriage my husband finally confessed he wants more than the two inches I leave for his message at the bottom of the cards we co-write. I am a full-blown hog when it comes to the written word. I am grateful he finally told me because he is a wonderful, expressive writer and his words deserve to hold a space of their own. "Make space for others" will be my holiday mantra this year.

How can you give freedom and space to the personality of those you love?

See others as who they are now

William Jonathan Steadman Medeiros (1997-2017)

"We knew Will was awesome at birth – his first word was 'ball' after all; but, as somewhat mediocre parents at best, we were flabbergasted by his abundant achievements and recognitions that way, way outreached his genetics in this short but extraordinarily rich life. For most of primary school, he aspired to be a rabbit (and developed a self-induced twitch as preparation). His timing was rarely off."

While Will's obituary is infused with humour, it ends on a more serious note. *"His aspirations having evolved from rabbit; he was hoping to become a lawyer. It was already beginning with his placing second in the 2016 C.L.A.U.S.E. Undergraduate Mock Trials Canada competition."*

Will's parents, who lost their son when he was 19 years old, convey their adoration for his quirky childhood persona. They acknowledge that he had enough talent to fuel his dream, but their focus remains on who he was, and still is, to them and the people who loved him.

Many of us lament the things we might have become if we had tried a little harder or if circumstance hadn't changed our trajectory. When we focus on who someone is, rather than who they have the potential to become, we are saying "you are more than enough, exactly as you are."

> *Can you find awe in all that is ordinary about the people you love, and choose to see them for who they are now rather than what you hope they become?*

Be a source of information

Jean Forbes Bowland (1926-2010)

"A dictionary and an atlas were always close at hand."

Jean loved to learn and shared this love with many young people by teaching them to read. She avidly followed current events, appreciated classical music, opera and ballet and *"relished conversations on many subjects."*

She must have been an incredible source of information on many topics long before Google. By having a dictionary and atlas close at hand Jean would have been able to extol information when it carried greatest value — in its moment of relevance.

Our boys went to a public Montessori elementary school. Dr. Maria Montessori believed that children learn better when parents and educators let them focus on what interests them. If they are getting excited about multiplication beads, they are encouraged to work with them until lunch hour. If they have latched onto word boxes, they are given the freedom to nestle in and word away. When we have resources close at hand, or as in Jean's case we are the resource, we can support interest, awe and learning on the spot.

What can you keep close at hand to feed the enthusiasm and interest of a young person?

Gifts you can't wrap

DECEMBER

Memories are not borne by extravagant gifts or fancy table linen. Most of us would agree that the greatest gifts can't be wrapped. You can't even touch them, but you can sense, sometimes in retrospect, you've been gifted something valuable. And best of all, you can regift them again and again.

The Retail Council of Canada says the average Canadian spends $792 on gifts in December. These purchases require an average of six trips to physical stores and seven visits to online retailers. None of the gifts noted in this chapter require waiting in line at the cash register, wracking your brain to remember a password or a pin number. And none of them come with an unwelcome credit card bill in January. They will keep on giving long after the small parts break and the batteries run out in the gifts you took the time to wrap.

There's nothing wrong with store-bought gifts — it's an accepted language of affection. But often, the gifts we truly remember don't come in fancy wrapping with a shiny bow.

In the thousands of obituaries I've read over the span of two decades, I don't remember a single one that focused on a person's possessions. In the end, what matters most is the small threads that connect us, that bind us together like strands of rope.

The best gifts are made with a few remarkable moments on ordinary days. Moments that help us feel seen and cherished, and provide a sense of belong. What matters most are our stories and the way they are intertwined in unexpected ways.

The following gifts are piled high to remind us that the best gifts can't be wrapped and never go out of style.

Model strength

Joan Martin Waterous (d. 2015)

*"In 1967 she returned to Toronto (with four children),
embarking on a series of entrepreneurial ventures, including
running a bar near City Hall and setting up a serviced
office complex at the Harbour-front, while simultaneously
qualifying for an M.A. in Consumer Studies on full
scholarship. Not bad for a single mother in the 1970s and
80s."*

When Joan gave her children advice to help them navigate
"the big and scary decisions in life" she had her own life to draw
upon for inspiration; *"follow your passions, listen to your gut and
put your family first."* The writer concedes, *"And, of course, she
was always right."* She encouraged each of her four children to
pursue their own path even when that meant building a life far
away from where she raised them. And so she became *"the glue*

of a family spread thousands of miles across multiple countries and time zones."

My mom was a single mom with five kids, so Joan's strength resonates with me. Mom and I insulated our small attic together when I was 12. Together we learned how to swing a hammer to secure a sub-floor over the sea of cotton-candy pink. When we finished the job we were smug and very, very itchy. That was the moment I decided a partner-in-life was an option, not a necessity. I can imagine that Joan's kids — and many people with capable single parents — have been shaped and empowered by watching their single parent in action.

> *What life experiences have you had that modelled strength? Can you share your story and enable others to draw strength from your experiences?*

Create a tradition

The Honorable James Bonham Strange Southey (1926-2016)

"...The annual Southey carol-singing party that he initiated in 1971 is a tradition loved by so many and replicated across the country."

Jim started a tradition with family and friends in his living room and the ripple effect will be felt for decades to come. Music was a thread that wove through every stage of his life, including singing hymns as a youth and attending Broadway musicals with his father. In his last years, when it became more difficult for Jim to put thoughts into words, *"lyrics expressed what he could not."* And yet this tradition he started will continue to give voice to something that James valued deeply; bringing people together to bask in the camaraderie of music.

I remember an ordinary morning at my friend's home when I was in Grade 10. The mystery home-schooled family they often spoke of showed up with instruments tucked in cases. This family of four unloaded and tuned violins without exchanging a word, and then broke into music around the piano. My friend's family members emerged from their bedrooms and joined, one at a time, until her home shook with the vibration. From that day on I vowed to build a home that knew music.

Although it's sporadic and often out of tune, my husband and I have made that wish come true.

What do you enjoy doing that could become a tradition if you shared it with others?

Put a new spin on a classic game

Maurice H.L. Pryce (1913-2003)

"He created a family tradition, perhaps characteristic of his personal philosophy, of Collaborative Scrabble — the main aim is, within the rules, to maximize the overall score rather than to beat the other players."

Maurice was invited to become a professor of physics at Oxford University at the ripe age of 32. His academic work focused on interpreting the magnetic properties of atoms, but his interest and knowledge extended into many branches of physics and his students were put to work tackling a wide range of topics. His appreciation for the value of teamwork, the sum being greater than the parts, was embodied in his version of Scrabble which valued the collective score of the team over that of the individual.

In addition to gifting a new game to his family, Maurice also modelled the value of changing rules in the name of invention.

What new spin can you give to a classic game that embodies what you value?

Show up and be present

Hilda Amy MacQuarrie (1921- 2006)

*"Thanks for letting me win at checkers, for making meals,
clothes, happiness. Thanks for the funny accents, the
swimming lessons, the winter walks, the glamour girl smiles,
the odd fits of fury. Thanks for knowing the names of all the
wildflowers, for helping with the fort, with the math, with
the play rehearsals."*

This is a gratitude journal that grew in the heart of Hilda's son.
I love knowing that a childhood of ordinary moments can be
strung together to create an extraordinary bond. I also appreciate
the reminder that a few extra seconds here and there (to offer the
name of a wildflower, for example) makes a lasting impression
on a child.

My husband and I had a brief but poignant interaction with a
stranger when I was busting at the seams with my first pregnancy.
The man whose son was grown and had "flown the nest" looked

at us and said "all you need to do is take them home and give them lots of love." I suspect we looked a bit rattled for him to spontaneously offer up this unsolicited advice, and it was just what we needed. To this day when I fret about being too firm, not tender enough, or wishing I had listened more attentively to our kids, I remind myself of his words and am reassured because at the end of each day they know they are loved.

Can you close the parenting book and just love your kids in whatever form that may take?

Home is the people, not the place

Nicholas Arnold Duquette Owens (1995-2020)

Nick lived his life in our small house, surrounded by a tight-knit clan of other loving, generous families in the Beach neighbourhood of Toronto. He was intensely loyal to his family. When Nick was the youngest of three, and the family moved from a two to a four-bedroom house, the siblings refused to decamp from their shared room."

Some of us find ourselves living life as if it were a board game. We start at "go" with nothing, and then incrementally collect money and material goods until someone says "you win." Getting a bigger property, or more properties, is the underlying goal. (That and staying out of jail.) I can imagine the excited flurry of questions from Nick's parents when they showed their big new home to their three kids for the first time. "Which room do you want? The one with a view of the oak tree or the one with the big closet?" Did they dot their enthusiasm with "You finally have enough space for a desk in your room!" We can imagine that Nick and his siblings flummoxed their parents when they opted to continue to cram into the same bedroom. Nick reminded them, and now he has reminded us, that bricks and mortar do not make the home. Home is the people living in it.

In my early childhood home one of the greatest treats was sandwiching between two of my older sisters on the floor of their shared bedroom. They would pull their foam mattresses off their toe-to-toe-beds, and we'd all line up side by each. It didn't bother me one iota that I'd slip between the cracks of the two foamies. We'd sing "roll over, roll over, they all rolled over and one rolled out…" and we'd talk until my brain would fall asleep but my mouth kept moving. As someone whose home went from enveloping a family of seven to a family of two (mom and me) at the age of nine, I know that Nick shared something exquisite with his siblings.

Is there something bigger that you are working towards? Are you willing to stop and consider if bigger will really be better?

Be a strong foundation

Edward R. Gosselin (1942-2009)

> *"Ed married the love of his life and best friend, Jeannette Brown, in 1969. They were inseparable and an incredible team, eventually settling on an acreage near Melfort, Saskatchewan where they raised four children. Ed had an unbridled exuberance for his children and would do anything to help them succeed. He instilled a strong sense of values in his children by the way he lived his life. He was always supportive and available, gave generously of his time and guided each one in finding their own way. Most recently, the love for Ed's children could also be seen in his joy and enthusiasm for his grandchildren who lovingly knew him as 'Grandpa Goose' the silly song singer, the creative story reader, and the outdoor enthusiast."*

Ed studied agriculture, an interest stemming from his work alongside his father on the Saskatchewan farm of his childhood.

After working as an agricultural representative for several years his strong sense of social justice led him to law school. After just five years in law practice he was called to the bench as a judge of the Provincial Court of Saskatchewan where he served for 28 years. Despite the enormity of this honour it is noted in his obituary that *"Ed's proudest accomplishments were the lives he most closely influenced, supported and cherished: those of his family."*

Providing a solid foundation for your kids, be it as two parents who live together, two parents who live apart or one parent who loves enough for two, is a priceless gift.

> *Who provided a strong foundation for you? What foundation are you leaving for those who come after you?*

Create an original

Dr. Melville Joseph Swartz (1912-2006)

> *"Mel cherished his wife and family. He composed a lullaby for his young children and sang it to them every night."*

Mel was from the old-school of doctoring: long hours, house calls, and lifelong relationships with many patients. Yet he carved out this tradition of singing to his three children while serving as the head of Urology at two hospitals.

"He worked in British Columbia's interior and northern goldmines, in Alaska and on the Empress of Canada to Shanghai. In the Second World War, a Major in the Royal Army Medical Corps, he moved by horse, ship, rail, foot and parachute through India, Burma and the South Pacific."

Mel may have gleaned inspiration for song and poetry from the remote and exotic places he worked and served. And when he returned to Canada to marry and build a life with his wife Ruby, he continued to find awe and inspiration around him. His keen appreciation for the minute details of beauty continued into his final decade. *"At 91, he saw his first pileated woodpecker, and at 93, a rare whooping crane!"*

If you happen upon the bench in Assiniboine Park (Winnipeg) with this poem written by Mel Swartz at the age of 17, you, too, will experience one of Mel's originals. When he wrote this poem his goal was to include as many enormous words in one piece as possible. His teacher didn't fail him, but she *"looked at him askance."* Mel thought this hilarious.

Hail O hyperdiaphonous and supralustrous orb of day In whose effulgent beams, lusorious insects romp and play...

We know that Mel's lullaby is a precious memory for his adult children because they made note of it in his obituary. I didn't compose a lullaby for our boys, but I often sang them a bedtime song we had heard at Parent-Child Mother Goose. Come bedtime I was always too spent to recall the lyrics, so I made them up instead. I didn't compose a lullaby for our boys, but thanks to Mel I feel pretty great about singing a one-of-a-kind bedtime song to them.

> *If you don't have Mel's talent for music, what original creation can you offer to soothe someone else? A hand-made quilt? A unique recipe? A portrait? A fairytale?*

Pick up the slack

Evelyn Mitchell (1933-2019)

*"We were posted to Halifax in the early 1970s. Just in time
for my mother to help care for her father-in-law. In return
for borrowing their equipment, mum offered her time to
Red Cross to drive patients to treatments and appointments.
Only the service didn't extend to Dartmouth where we lived.
As this was unacceptable to mum, she received permission
to establish Red Cross transportation for Dartmouth out of
our home. She marshalled a small contingent of volunteer
drivers who borrowed our car or used their own. Eventually
she secured the support of the Dartmouth Golden K's
(Kiwanis) who generously donated a vehicle and several
more drivers. The service continued from our home until
my parents retired."*

Most people complain when there is no service for what they
need. Evelyn was the type of person who got busy and figured

out how to provide it. She leapt into action to fill the gap in service that *other people* needed. Her infectious enthusiasm (and perhaps a twisted arm or two) led to others joining her mission. Evelyn created a service that continues to give, even after she is gone. "*She would be the last to believe she left a legacy. Yet the number of lives changed is legion.*"

> *Are you going to be the complainer or the (arm-twisting) visionary? What gap can you fill?*

Preserve your culture

Yvonne Joe (1937-2019)

"Yvonne was a shíshálh language champion, one of the last fluent speakers of the shíshálh Nation. She has been working for the last 40-plus years to preserve and document the language with the shíshálh Translation Group. She was also one of the first shíshálh language teachers, teaching at the Sechelt Elementary and the Native Environment School up in Jervis Inlet."

Forty years is a long time for someone to work on any project. The value of what Yvonne did goes beyond preserving and documenting a language. By devoting half of her life to this work she demonstrated how deeply important she felt it was. Dedication of this magnitude would only serve to add to the value of the shíshálh language in the eyes of others. Add that to her obvious gift, the documentation of the shíshálh language which will continue to strengthen the connection of her people with their elders, their roots and their identity.

What can you share with others to honour and help preserve your culture, be it a language, a story or a family recipe?

Food as a love language

Celestina Belluz (1922-2020)

"Celestina expressed her deep love of family through her meals. She'd set the table every night for a multi-course feast, one that her husband, kids and grandkids would eagerly anticipate."

When we think of veterans of the Second World War, we often picture men in uniform and to them a great debt is owed. And often as not, what kept these soldiers going through the hard times was a tattered picture in their coat pocket or a hand-written letter in the barracks. For many, thoughts of home spurred them on and for Gino Belluz, it was a young woman named Celestina in the small town of Azzano Decimo, Italy.

The two fell in love, but their plans to marry were upended by the start of the war. Gino was drafted in 1940, and Celestina stayed behind, while bombs rained down around their homestead.

When the war ended, in 1945, Gino returned to Azzano and the two were married.

Celestina's cooking was remarkable. Her hearth, and eventually modern stoves, helped create a return to normalcy, and a place for people to gather.

Upon relocating to Canada after the war, she cooked meals for boarders as a way to provide for the family financially and to create a haven for others in Toronto's Italian community. The number of plates she set around the family table grew over the years, and her lovingly-prepared dishes were the centrepiece for three generations of Belluzs'.

"The table would fill with home-made gnocchi and wine, involtini or chicken cacciatore, perfectly seasoned vegetables grown from her farm and garden, always followed by a cheese plate and fresh fruit. She relished hosting big celebrations — Christmases with mortadella-stuffed capons and home-made panettone; Easters with raisin-specked frittole."

In sharing traditional recipes and customs with her family, most likely learned from her own mother, Celestina expressed her love and provided a connection to their shared Italian heritage.

> *What favourite recipe(s) to you prepare to express your love? What dish, prepared at the hands of another, serves as reminder that you are loved?*

Teach resourcefulness

John Sherman Bleakney (1928-2019)

"To impart to us kids his enthusiasm for the ocean and diving, he painstakingly made us child-size wetsuits (these were the days before kids' wetsuits were sold in Canadian Tire!), using sheets of thick neoprene rubber and rubber glue (the smell of which permeated our house when he was working on them, taking out a few of our brain cells, no doubt), measuring us up, cutting the pieces from the rubber sheets, and expanding the suits by gluing in strips of rubber each year as we grew. The snorkelling trips with dad off the shores of Nova Scotia were a highlight of our childhood, swimming through schools of ink-squirting squid, over fields of sand dollars, and even thrilling nighttime expeditions through glowing diatomaceous bioluminescence where the ocean left trails of light all around us."

Sherman was known as one of the "fathers of Canadian herpetology" (the branch of zoology concerned with reptiles and amphibians). His actions underline how much he prized time with his children and his intense desire to allow them to experience the awe of ocean life. He also showed his children that you can refuse to be limited by what is available and instead make available what you need. His loving act of making neoprene suits for his children by hand speaks volumes about what Sherman valued, and his children heard this message loud and clear.

I consider being resourceful my super power. I learned it from my mother, a single mom of five children. She learned it from my grandfather who grew up in an orphanage in England. My mom was unabashed about pulling still-useful things from the garbage can of a stranger. Much to my horror she would often knock on the stranger's door to ask for permission to take it, at least partially motivated by the opportunity to explain how she planned to use the item. Their accolades for her ingenuity almost always followed.

For Grade 12 graduation I nailed a rubber door stopper into the bottom of my pumps to replace a missing heel. Nothing gives me more satisfaction than fixing something with what I have on hand.

My grandfather saved all the handles, hinges and knobs from everything he discarded in his lifetime. The result is an entire wall of jars filled with hardware representing every decade in the last century. He has been gone for three decades, but when I am at our family cabin on Lake Winnipeg I take my morning coffee into his unaltered workshop. There, I admire his rusty shrine to resourcefulness lit by a small stream of sunlight revealing varying patinas of brass, copper and steel.

Can you get really resourceful to make possible something that seems impossible?

Be the impetus for a new law

James Gordon Cook (1926-2019)

Gord "never met a dog he didn't like, never met a dog he didn't stop and have a conversation with, a trait he has passed on to his sons."

According to his sons, his best financial move was the purchase of a mutt named Dino — for five bucks — (leash and collar included), thanks to an ad on a grocery store bulletin board. Despite the cheap price, Gord got more than he bargained for. *"Dino's propensity to fertilize neighbour's lawns and impregnate their lassies resulted in Stoop & Scoop and Canine Planned Parenting by-laws being enacted in Toronto."*

Sometimes what we "leave behind" becomes an unintended legacy — a new law. We all know someone responsible for the "code brown" posters at the community swimming pool. And if that's your legacy, celebrate. You've definitely left your mark.

What bold move have you made that might have inspired a new law?

Keep telling stories

Andrew Bentham Batten (1963-2019)

"If you had the honour and privilege of knowing this man, you would know that he would not want his family and friends to mourn him for too long — he would instead ask them to make sure they were their best selves, read more, travel more, be kind to each other, and enjoy this amazing world in which we live; and, above all, keep telling your stories, Andrew was fond of saying that people listen when you tell them your stories."

As a teacher, performer and playwright Andrew knew first-hand the power of story-telling. He entertained, engaged, conveyed information and inspired with stories. And because stories will never have an expiration date, neither will the people who write them, tell them or stand squarely in the spotlight of them.

Andrew *"was thrilled to learn"* that a play he produced in 1995 is going to be remounted in 2020. *"Andrew loved Shakespeare and he wrote this delicious, irreverent prequel of 'Romeo and Juliet' using iambic pentameter."* Andrew's story will continue to be told with the same passion and colour with which he infused it.

My husband was 21 years-old when his father, Victor, died. My Dad died just last year. But it's Victor our boys speak of as if they saw him just yesterday. Through stories he is still the 13 year-old boy who was stripped of his childhood the moment he ran into the woods of Croatia to become a Partisan soldier to fight Nazi oppression. He is the young man in his 20s who dove through barbed fences under gunfire to escape Tito's rule, and then started life anew in Canada. The dad who, rather than admonishment and shame, laughed while watching his son smash through the deck with his new (16-year-old) driving skills. He is - and always will be - the man with flowing hair and a Hollywood-worthy smile that could have won the heart of any Thunder Bay beauty, but saw the true gem in their grandmother Bridgette. It is thanks to the power of story that Victor is alive in the mind and hearts of our boys.

Photo albums and scrapbooks have their role, but what stories can you tell to keep the memory of a loved one alive?

Afterword

Timeless gifts

The life stories of those who share space in this book offer us gifts — inspiration, insights, and interesting perspectives. If you received any gifts while reading this book, they are yours to keep. Admire them. Play with them. Re-gift them freely.

The newspapers that conveyed these life stories may fade and turn yellow, but their gifts can last a lifetime. They are timeless.

After doing an interview on CBC *Maritime Noon* in January 2020, I received an email from a man in Nova Scotia. He heard the interview and wanted to share a clipping he had tucked away.

"I read and clipped Jack Lang's obit from The Globe and Mail in 1999 because I found his life quite interesting and the obit dedication lovely. I didn't know the man but loved the story about the milk delivery gone amuck, lol. Perhaps because my father and uncle and their father were milkmen in the Moncton NB Area. Maybe it was the impish grin on Jack's face that captivated my attention."

— Bruce Milton, Mineville, Nova Scotia

Twenty-one years later, Jack's obituary — and his life story — still live on in Bruce's home. He lives on in my hands, too, as I hold the same obituary I had clipped more than two decades ago. Bruce's email is poignant because it identifies what it was about the obituary that prompted him to walk over to a drawer, take out a pair of scissors and snip the obituary for safe-keeping.

I have since met (by email and phone) the very lovely Carol-Ann Lang, Jack Lang's daughter and the person who crafted this beautiful obituary. She was deeply touched that her writing introduced her father to another person on the other coast of Canada 6,000 kilometres away. She was moved to learn that Bruce Milton felt a strong enough connection to Jack to pull out his obituary 20 years later and email it to a stranger.

Timely gifts

Many times I have picked up an obituary in my "favourites" file, only to find myself more drawn to the words of the obituary beside it. The one I glanced over years before. Yet now I feel certain those words found me at just the right time. Reading the obituaries is like that. The things that we are looking for have a way of finding us. In this way, they are timely.

In my 20s I appreciated stories about people who sopped up life experiences and found love later in life. Today, I am drawn to reflections of a parenting style that invites me to make small shifts. Years from now (if I'm that lucky), I will scour for tips on how to be a kick-butt grandparent and unearth new interests.

If you already read obits, welcome to the wonderful club that you are a member of (and, like me, probably didn't even know existed). It turns out there are far more of us than I thought. I have received letters from others across Canada and beyond who have been reading obituaries for years, several longer than I have. Many are secret readers who hide the evidence. Others are celebratory and text photos of their favourites to friends. If you have not indulged, it's not too late to start, and nothing is more timely than the present. There are many things we could run out of in this world, but life stories are not one of them.

The present is a gift

There is only one thing better than reading a person's life story after they are gone, and that is listening to them tell their story while they are still with us.

There are many people — both near and far away — who have stories to tell. Don't wait until they are gone to receive the gifts hidden in their storied past or present. Capture their offerings while you still have the opportunity to steep in the goodness with them. If you're not sure where to start with questions, I invite you to pull from mine at www.Obittersweet.com #Save Their Story Project (also on Instagram and Pinterest). Listening to someone's story is a gift to both the listener and the story-teller.

One final gift

There is one more gift that can be found in reading obituaries or listening to the stories of others. It comes from asking yourself one very important question. Imagine holding a newspaper and turning to the obituary section. There, instead of the face of a stranger *your* photo stares back at you in black and white. It's *your* name that follows with a few short paragraphs to sum up your life.

> *What stories capture the essence of who you are and what you value most? How do you want others to remember you?*

You may be surprised at how your answer shapes the days, months and years in front of you.

Ode to the two-leggeds

ACKNOWLEDGEMENTS

To my three "boys" – you rock. You encouraged me to close my door and opened it only to fill my coffee cup. My love and respect for you moves me to be a better human. Thanks for not thinking me completely mad for turning to the dead for gifts to help me on my way.

To my outrageously capable Mom (Aynslie), thank you for teaching me that being conventional is overrated and that unconditional love rules. Bottoms up to my four trail-blazing sisters who have populated our family tree with seriously awesome humans. Lynne, thanks for embracing the mayhem with love, and Dad (Rod), for setting the bar high in every way possible.

Thank you Edgar Cowan. Your phone call the day after my personal essay was published in *The Globe and Mail* asking "Can you turn this into a book?" sent me to the moon. And then back again to start writing. Howard Aster, and the Mosaic Press team, thank you for lending your wisdom, garnered over 44 years of publishing in Canada's independent book industry. Your commitment to continuing to give rise to Canadian voices is significant.

Constance Mears helped me reach up and grab my disparate swirling thoughts and pin them down to take the shape of this book. She gave clarity to concept, polished my words, and wrapped them with a bow. I extend my gratitude to Crystal Stranaghan (and the Creatrixes) for fuelling my brainwaves over the past decade, my book club girls (18 years and counting!) for keeping my nose in books and my pen in hand and, of course, the one and only E.

To my advisors: indigenous multi-disciplinary artist and classroom poetry partner, Chris Bose; philosophy buff and seer of meaning in depths void of light, Shane Bursey; long-time book club cohort and voracious reader, Karen Niedbala; Carleton journalism school sidekick, troublemaker with a cause, and author, Carreen Maloney; psychologist and community health scientist (and friend since Grade 3), Dr. Rob Santos; and, an assistant professor at Thompson Rivers University widely recognized for her dogged advocacy to improve quality of life for individuals with disabilities and their families, Dr. Nan Stevens.

Thanks to my sister Kerri for giggling beside me in bed when I recited obits from my scraggly file of favourites during my last pilgrimage to visit our Dad before he died last year. You confirmed the value of these "obittersweets" and helped to lighten our hearts.

Tanya Miniely, you empowered me and gave vision to my love of obituaries from the middle of your life sandwich while caring for your Dad and being the loudest parent on the sidelines. Thank you to the many people who have coaxed me to write my heart out. I'm grateful for those who have consistently encouraged me from unexpected places, including Ellen Jacobson, Marion Dyck Whitford, Tania Cameron-Inglis and the Grade 3 substitute teacher who took this solid B student aside and told her she would "be a great writer one day."

Ode to the wordsmiths

OBITUARY CREDITS

written by / publication / date

Ablett, Albert (Ab) Arthur .... son Dave Ablett
Kamloops This Week, Jan. 7, 2016

Ainley, June Marie Rosaleen Kidman... granddaughter Monica de la Villardière
The Globe and Mail, Feb. 17, 2019

Alexander, Dr. Skaria .... Victoria (wife) and sons Arun and Abe
Times Colonist, Jun. 22, 2019

Alexandrowicz, Professor George .... The Alexandrowicz family
The Globe and Mail, Dec. 7, 2019

Ambery, Aida Maria... husband Mark Ambery
The Globe & Mail, June 13,2015

Armour, Sascha.. son Douglas Armour
The Globe and Mail, Aug. 5, 2017

Atkinson, Charles "Stormin" Norman .... daughter Hallie MacDonald
Kamloops This Week April 30, 2019

Cook, James Gordon..................................... sons Stephen, Alan and Glenn Cook
The Globe and Mail, Oct. 26, 2019

Cooper, Charles William "Bill".. wife Marj Cooper
Kamloops This Week May 23, 2019

Currie, Martha Bernice Home...sons Mike and Jay Currie
The Globe and Mail Dec. 7, 2019

Davis, Burnice Lucille.. granddaughter Gwen Davis
Kamloops This Week, Jan. 30, 2017

Demidoff, George Robert...wife Carol Demidoff
Kamloops This Week, Nov. 21, 2019

Doherty, Catherine.. sister Elizabeth Doherty
The Globe and Mail, Nov. 2, 2019

Duguay, Herbert Mosses...daughter Shawn Bird
www.shawnbird.com, July 25, 2015

Ellison, Lorna Leslie brother / sister-in-law Walter Thomas and Ellen Mary Mills
The Globe and Mail, Feb. 10, 2018

Ennis, Michael........... wife Joanne Ennis and brother-in-law Michael Rutherford
The Globe and Mail, Apr. 7, 2018

Fonso, Dennis James (alias Foxy).......................wife Michele Fitzmaurice Fonzo
Thunder Bay Chronicle Journal, Apr. 13, 2019

Forster, James Henry................................ children Suzanne and Andrew Forster
The Globe and Mail, Sep. 28, 2019

Foulds, Derek Macdonald.. daughter Rosemary Foulds
The Globe and Mail, Nov. 23, 2019

Godden, Barbara "Jean"................. children Tim, Heather and Barbara Godden
The Globe and Mail, July 9, 2016

Gollnow, Dieter Ernst...........................The Gollnows (Edda, Angie, Sabrina and
granddaughters Sofia and Juliette)
The Globe and Mail, Nov. 2, 2019

Gordon, Ilse.. daughter, Gisèle Gordon
The Globe and Mail, June 28, 2016

Gosselin, Edward R..... wife Jeanette; children Marc, Hillary, Colin and Brendan
The Globe and Mail, June 17, 2009

Gosselin, Roland .... daughter Tanya Miniely
Weekend Yellowknifer, Aug. 7, 2020

Gould, George Ernest ....children Anne Louise Gould and John Gould
The Globe and Mail, Jan. 20, 2017

Groll, Dr. Aubrey.. The family of Aubrey Groll
The Globe and Mail, Feb. 24, 2018

Gropper, Zora Elka..... children Risa Levine, Miriam Mitchell and Peter Gropper
The Globe and Mail, Oct. 26, 2019

Hamer-Jackson, Diana .... daughters Vicki and Loni Hamer-Jackson
Kamloops This Week, Nov. 21, 2019

Hansen, Poul-Erik Skovsbo .... daughter Pia D. Hansen
The Globe and Mail, Nov. 23, 2019

Hawkins, William ....friend Roy MacSkimming
The Globe and Mail on Jul. 9, 2016

Hawryliw, Eileen Mary .... the Hawryliw family
The Globe and Mail, Feb. 10, 2018

Helfinger, Johanna .... daughter Nancy McCormack (d.) and son Michael
Helfinger
The Globe and Mail, Oct. 6, 2019

Helfinger, Rudolf. daughter Nancy McCormack (d.) and son Michael Helfinger
The Globe and Mail on May 6, 2014

Hincenbergs, Maria-Louise .... daughter Frances Hincenbergs
Toronto Star, Oct. 19, 2019

Hollick-Kenyon, Timothy Hugh daughter Susan Hollick-Kenyon with edits from
Sandie and Tim Hollick-Kenyon ....
The Globe and Mail, Nov. 24, 2019

Iribarne, Agripina Palade..daughter Gabriela Iribarne
The Globe and Mail, Nov. 30, 2019

Jansen, Dr. Margaret .... Clifford, Carlyle and Mary-Ann Jansen
Toronto Star, May 26, 2018

Joe, Yvonne........................children, Bruce, Cindy, Sandra, Tim, Nancy and Zena
Coast Reporter, Feb. 1, 2019

Joy, Michael L.G. .... brother John Andras
The Globe and Mail, July 13, 2020

Laird, Zachary Schylore... mother Dana Goodman
Kamloops Daily News, May 6, 2010

Lang, John (Jack) Edwin .... daughter Carol-Ann Lang
The Globe and Mail, Dec 4, 1999

Langford, J. Alexander...................................daughters Anne and Jane Langford
The Globe and Mail, July 28, 2019

Lyons, Keiko Margaret ....daughter Ruth Shizuka Lyons
The Globe and Mail, Dec. 8, 2019

MacKay, Patricia Marilyn..the family of Pat MacKay
The Globe and Mail, Oct. 5, 2019

MacKay, Roderick Milne .... son Alan MacKay
Victoria Times-Colonist, Apr. 10, 2012

MacNicol, Hugh Alexander ....sons Scott, David & Robert MacNicol
The Globe and Mail, Sept. 29, 2019

MacQuarrie, Hilda Amy .... son David MacQuarrie
The Globe and Mail, Dec. 11, 2006

Marker, Frederick Joseph ....Frederick Joseph Marker
The Globe and Mail, Nov. 23, 2019

Martin, David Grant .... wife Patricia Barss
Winnipeg Free Press on Oct 12, 2019

McGee, R.A. Gordon .... brother Tim McGee
The Globe and Mail, Aug. 10, 2019

McLeod, Roderick James .... The McLeod Family
The Globe and Mail, Dec. 7, 2019

Medeiros, William Jonathan Steadman ....mother Laura Coulman
The Globe and Mail, Feb. 2, 2017

Mitchell, Evelyn .... daughter Caron (Mitchell) Wood
The Chronicle Herald, Oct. 13, 2019

Moad, George S.B. .... wife Louise Lang
The Globe and Mail, Nov. 10, 2019

Moffat, Margaret Elizabeth .... children Susan Brenciaglia, Ann and Norman Moffat
The Globe and Mail, Dec. 29, 2018

Nokleberg, Margaret Jordis .... son Andrew Nikiforuk
The Globe and Mail, Nov. 17, 2019

Olljum, Irene Gunhild ....children Alar J. Rudolf Olljum and LIlian Olljum
Vancouver Sun, October 26, 2019

Owens, Nicholas Arnold Duquette .... mother Laurel Duquette
The Globe and Mail, May 30, 2020

Portnuff, Paul .... nephew Drew Berman
Winnipeg Free Press, Feb. 5, 2010

Pryce, Maurice Henry Lecorney .... Copyright: Roger Elliott and John Sanders
The Independent, London; The Globe and Mail, Sep. 9, 2003

Ross Sturdee, Doris Mary . son Oakland Ross, with memories from her children and grandchildren
Toronto Star, Jul. 10, 2017

Sellers, Rev. Walter (Paddy) ....daughter Sandra Kuelz
The Globe and Mail, Oct. 19, 2019

Sharp, Daryl Leonard Merle ....the children of Daryl Sharp
The Globe and Mail, Oct. 19, 2019

Sheppard, Patrick .... wife Linda Sheppard and and daughter Victoria Sheppard
The Globe and Mail, Nov. 23, 2019

Southey, The Honorable James Bonham Strange . children Peter Southey, Sally Southey and lifetime family friend Shelagh Speers
The Globe and Mail, July 30, 2016

Steiger, Ruby .... daughters Linda Steiger and Gertrude Kearns
The Globe and Mail, July 9, 2016

Stewart, Lynn Ann .... husband John Slavin
The Globe and Mail, Nov. 23, 2019

Swartz, Dr. Melville Joseph .... daughters Jill and Jo Swartz
Winnipeg Free Press, Nov 22, 2006

Swartz, Ruby .... daughters Jo and Jill Swartz
Winnipeg Free Press, Apr 1, 2010

Tudhope, Erie M. .... sons Hilton Tudhope, Beverley and Ian
The Globe and Mail, July 18, 2020

Umar, Aisha Tara .... the Umar family
The Globe and Mail, Nov. 29, 2019

Vallilee, Kenneth Joseph Alexander .... daughter Summer Innanen
The Globe and Mail, Oct. 5, 2019

Vosu, Dr. Dagmar .... daughter Helen Vosu
The Globe and Mail, Sept. 28, 2019

Voyatzis, Irene Mavis .... children Paul Voyatzis and Athena Westlaken
The Globe and Mail, Dec. 8, 2019

Wanless, Annette Elizabeth .... the Wanless family .
The Globe and Mail, Oct. 5, 2019

Washburn, Irene .... son Don Washburn .
The Globe and Mail, Oct. 18, 2014

Waterous, Joan Martin .... daughter Johanna Waterous .
Toronto Star, July 11, 2015

Watt, Mary Louise .... son Ian Watt .
The Globe and Mail, Nov. 23, 2019

Weldon, Ina Perry .... daughter Mardie J Weldon .
The Globe and Mail, July 11, 2017

Whittle, Edris .... Josephine Shannon Wilson and the family of Edris Whittle .
Toronto Star, Oct. 26, 2019

Winfield, Barbara Ann .... sisters Peg Kelly & Carol Deimling .
The Globe and Mail, Mar. 30, 2019

Wood, Jane S. .... son Tony Wood .
The Globe and Mail, Nov. 24, 2019

Woodyatt, William .... sister Mari-Jayne Woodyatt .
Toronto Star, Nov. 16, 2019

Sources

JANUARY

Richard, Joanne. "The new year's resolution revolution". torontosun.com. *Toronto Sun*, January 5, 2020.

Nadon, Suzanne. Book review of "The Brillig Trilogy by Daryl Sharp". Dream Network, January 1997.

Johnson, Sharon Dawn. Book review of "Who Am I, Really? by Daryl Sharp". C.G. Jung Society of Ottawa Newsletter, April 2000.

Walker, James W. St.G. "Black Canadians." The Canadian Encyclopedia. May 14, 2015.

FEBRUARY

Styles, Ruth. "Looking for love? Try the office!". dailymail.com. *The Daily Mail* on-line newspaper. September 29, 2013.

Smith, Jacquelyn. "My office romance turned into a marriage - Here are 13 rules for dating a co-worker". www.independent.co.uk. *Business Insider*, January 25, 2016.

"The average time spent on mobile phones and social media increases in Canada." eye-in.com. Eye In Media, July 25, 2018.

MARCH

Devlin, Emma. "Irish Blessings and Prayers for Funerals." www.irishcentral.com. Irish Central, July 24, 2017.

APRIL

Cocozza, Paula. "Your younger sibling is funnier than you (at least that's what they say)" www.theguardian.com. The Guardian, January 28, 2015.

Cherkas, Lynn, Fran Hochberg, Alex J MacGregor, Harold Snieder and Tim D Spector. "Happy families: a twin study of humour". Twin Research and Genetic Epidemiology Unit, St Thomas' Hospital, London, UK. Cambridge University Press, Volume 3, pp. 17–22, February 1, 2000.

Shriners International. "Brotherhood" www.shrinersinternational.org. 2020

"The History of Writing in Scots" www.scotslanguage.com. *Scots Language Centre*, Perth.

Manninen, Sandra. "Social Laughter Triggers Endogenous Opioid Release in Humans". www.jneurosci.org. *Journal of Neuroscience* June 21, 2017

MAY

Smith, Daniel P. "Dollar Days: A Primer for the Five Busiest Dining Days of the Calendar Year." www.fsrmagazine.com. FSR Magazine, January 2014

Greier, Eric. "More Canadians living alone and without children census figures show." www.cbc.ca. CBC News, August 2, 2017.

JUNE

Griffin, R. Morgan. "Give your body a boost with laughter." www.webmd.com. Wed MD.

JULY

Immigration, Refugees and Citizenship. "Syrian Outcomes Report." www.canada.ca, June 2019

Thomas, Derrick. "Giving and volunteering among Canada's immigrants". www150.statcan.gc.ca. Statistics Canada, May 17, 2012.

Barr, Cathy and David Lasby. "30 Years of Giving in Canada: The Giving Behaviour of Canadians: Who gives, how and why?" www.sapg-acpdo.org. Rideau Hall Foundation, 2018.

Duffin, Erin. "Number of immigrants in Canada 2000-2019." www.statista.com, October 30, 2019.

"Launching the Poul Hansen Family Centre for Depression at Toronto Western Hospital". www.tgwhf.ca. Toronto General & Western Hospital Foundation newsletter.

"Children learned about the Holocaust from George Brady and Hana's Suitcase." cbc.ca. CBC The Sunday Edition, January 18, 2019.

Abedon, Emily Perlman. "Toddler Empathy." www.parents.com. *Parents Magazine.*

"One-On-One Interview with Aisha Umar." www.biotcanada.ca. *BIoT Canada* magazine for IT professionals, 1 September, 2010.

Evans, Lisa. "Why Choose Canada?" www.CanadianImmigrant.ca, May 27, 2013.

Macaluso, Grace. "More Women in Dealerships is just plain good for Business." www.canada.autonews.com. *Automotive News Canada,* November 12, 2018.

Seymour, Rhea, "Shifting Out of Neutral: The Automotive Industry." www.womenofinfluence.ca, *Women of Influence,* October 21, 2013.

Statistics Canada, Labour Force Suvey, December 2019. www150.statcan.gc.ca. January 1, 2020.

Edwards, Peter. "Canadian Scientists Take Aim at Big Bang Theory." thestar.com. *The Toronto Star,* February 19, 2015.

"Doctoral program enrolment and completion in Canada." Statistics Canada, October 17, 2008.

"Universidad de Buenos Aires (UBA) ranking." www.topuniversitites.com. QS World University Rankings.

Meehan, Hilda. "Petite Physician on Wheels Never Misses Call for Help". The Montreal Gazette, April 21, 1952

Banner, Sandra. "The solution for Canada's doctor shortage is abroad."www.thespec.com. The Hamilton Spectator. March 2, 2020.

Wong, Anne, and Lynne Lohfeld. "Recertifying as a doctor in Canada: international medical graduates and the journey from entry to adaptation". www.pubmed.ncbi.nlm.nih.gov, January 2008.

Statistics Canada. "Primary health care provideres 2019." www.150.statcan.gc.ca. October 22, 2020.

Graham, Lisa. "Remembering Professor George Alexandrowicz." www.law.queensu.ca. Queen's University, December 11, 2019.

"Select Selenium and Vitamin E Cancer Prevention Trial." Island Prostate Centre, Victoria, BC.

AUGUST

Generation status: Canadian born children of immigrants. Statistics Canada. 2011.

The Canadian Tai Chi Academy. www.canadiantaichiacademy.org.

Official website of the Friends of Algonquin Park. www.algonquinpark.on.ca.

Rieck, Thom. "10,000 steps a day: Too low? Too high?" mayoclinic.org. Mayo Clinic, March 23, 2020.

"The History of Instagram." www.instazood.com. May 17, 2020

A & E Televsion Networks, "Facebook Launches". www.history.com/this-day-in-history/facebook-launches-mark-zuckerberg. October 24, 2019.

SEPTEMBER

"The Marathon of Hope." The Terry Fox Foundation. www.terryfox.org.

"William Hawkins poetry collection featured on 'All in a Day." www.cbc.ca. CBC News, July 4, 2016.

"Remembering Ottawa's Historic Coffee Houses." heritageottawa.org. Heritage Ottawa, July 18, 2016.

Langston, Patrick. "Joni Mitchell, Hendrix, Lightfoot - Le Hibou "absolutely vital" to Ottawa's local music scene." ottawamagazine.com. *Ottawa Magazine,* March 29, 2017.

Canadian Cancer Society. *"Survival Statistics for Ovarian Cancer."* www.cancer.ca.

Thompson, Greg and Karen Greve Young. *"Cancer in Canada: Framing the Crisis and Previewing the Opportunity for Donors."* Charity Intelligence Canada. April 2011.

Middleton, J.W. and A Dayton, J Walsh, S B Rutkowski, G Leong & S Duong "Life expectancy after spinal cord injury: a 50-year study."www.nature.com. Spinal Cord, May 15, 2012.

OCTOBER

Zeidler, Maryse. "This Vancouver man will be the oldest qualified runner at the 2020 Boston Marathon." www.cbc.ca. CBC News, March 1, 2020.

Solan, Matthew. "Back to school: Learning a new skill can slow cognitive aging." www.health.harvard.edu. Harvard Health Publishing, Harvard Medical School, April 27, 2016.

"How does a roller coaster work? www.bbc.co.uk/bitesize/topics. British Broadcasting Corporation.

Holmes, Leonard. "How the 'Widowhood Effect' Puts Widows at Risk After a Spouse's Death." www.verywellmind.com. Very Well Mind, November 10, 2019.

NOVEMBER

Layous K, Nelson SK, Oberle E, Schonert-Reichl KA, Lyubomirsky S (2012) Kindness Counts: Prompting Prosocial Behavior in Preadolescents Boosts Peer Acceptance and Well-Being. PLoS ONE 7(12): e51380.

Otake, K., Shimai, S., Tanaka-Matsumi, J. et al. Happy People Become Happier through Kindness: A Counting Kindnesses Intervention. J Happiness Stud 7, 361–375 (2006).

Government of Canada Library and Archives. "Service files of the Second World War - War Dead, 1939-1947." bac-lac.gc.ca.

Grabish, Austin. "Man whose hobby was waving to drivers in Brokenhead dead at 73." www.cbc.ca. CBC News, Manitoba, Nov 24, 2018

Ebert, Roger. "Patton review". RogerEbert.com. March 17, 2002.

Institut national de santé publique du Québec. *"Registering and choosing a name for your child."* www.inspq.qc.ca/

DECEMBER

Retail Council of Canada. *"RCC Holiday Shopping Survey 2019."* www.retailcouncil.org. November 12, 2019.

Hamblin, James. "Buy Experiences, Not Things." www.theatlantic.com. The Atlantic, October 7, 2014.

About the author

TAMARA MACPHERSON VUKUSIC

Tamara has three "boys" aged 13, 15 and 49, and is the guardian of quirky second-hand dogs. Journalism and political science degrees from Carleton University paved the way for Tamara to serve as a voice for several not-for-profit organizations spanning

two decades. A writer and former TV show host, she collects and repairs old typewriters to lasso kids (and kids-at-heart) into spilling ink.

She has been a guest on CBC's *Maritime Noon*, CBC *Kamloops Daybreak*, CFJC-TV *Midday* and *24 Hours Late Night* CBC-TV. Her writing has appeared in *The Globe & Mail, Nunatsiaq News, Nunavut*

News, Kamloops Parents, Kamloops Momma, Moms with Apps, Kamloops Daily News and on *Medium. Obittersweet* is her first book.

She has lived in the prairies, the nation's capital and the high arctic but has built her permanent nest in Kamloops with her husband. Alan, and their two boys.

Check out my blog at www.obittersweet.com for more life lessons from the obituaries and for tips on harnessing words to honour a life well-lived.

#SaveTheirStoryProject on Pinterest and Instagram.